Stephen R. White

The Seeking Church:

A SPACE FOR ALL

the columba press

First published in 2009 by
the columba press
55A Spruce Avenue, Stillorgan Industrial Park,
Blackrock, Co Dublin

Cover by Bill Bolger
Origination by The Columba Press
Printed in Ireland by ColourBooks, Dublin

ISBN 978 1 85607 628 9

Table of Contents

Introduction   7

1.   Yesterday's Church   13

2.   The Valley of the Dry Bones   27

3.   The Faith of the Church   38

4.   Remodelling the Church   50

5.   'Bind us together, Lord'   63

6.   *Theologia Peregrinatii*   76

7.   *Experientia Peregrinatii*   91

8.   A Mutual Ministry   101

9.   A Space for All – Doctrine   111

10   A Space for All – Ethics   122

11. A Space for All – Risk   136

12. Of No Fixed Abode   150

Conclusion   160

Notes   165

Index of Names   169

Introduction

This book follows on very closely from the ideas expressed in *A Space for Belief* and *A Space for Unknowing*. Between them these two books represent an attempt to articulate a new way of doing theology (or perhaps more properly a re-discovery of an old but oft-neglected way of doing theology), based on an exploration first of the general function of theology, and secondly of the intrinsic nature of theology itself. In the course of this, it was initially argued that the function of theology is not to pin us down and constrain us within a prison of (usually outmoded) rigidly defined credal propositions and confessional formulae, but rather to create a 'space for belief' within which there is room for a multiplicity of approaches and a substantial divergence of opinion as to exactly how particular doctrinal points are to be interpreted.

Following on from this it was suggested that theology is, by its very nature, actually incapable (if used correctly) of tying us down in this way. For theology does not work with the tools of propositional certainty, but primarily with unknowing or *agnosis*, and with a powerfully relational approach to faith. Its formulae are not timeless and immutable and somehow 'correct' definitions of God or of anything else, but provisional models and pictures which help to guide and shape our faith, and which are subject to perpetual re-evaluation and revision. This is an estimate of theology which Timothy Kinahan expresses particularly succinctly:

> Christian statements need to take account of who we are, where we are, and where we come from; they need to be related to the experience of the generation in question. Better

words may be found to articulate the Christian faith for a new generation. All statements of doctrine must be provisional. Otherwise they risk fossilisation.[1]

Indeed, since writing the previous two books, I have been both interested and encouraged to notice a growing number of theological writers and commentators coming independently to similar conclusions. Thus, for example, Gerhard Sauter, in a major study of dogmatics, writes that: '... any profound and far-reaching correction of former theological statements is possible ... No dogma is formulated for all time or for eternity ... Theology is a pilgrim theology.'[2]

This brings us to the need for the present book, which is related equally to the directions I have been suggesting that theology ought to move in, and to the current situation of the institutional churches. Both theology and that situation would appear to require some kind of a change in the church's self-understanding, and, as will be argued, a radical one at that. As I wrote several years ago in a paper issued by the Department of Theological Questions of the Irish Inter-Church Meeting:

If these features of pluralism, relativism and provisionality reflect at all accurately the face of society today, then presumably the church that ministers to and witnesses in such a climate needs to be one that is capable of responding to these trends ... Thus the question immediately arises: Is the church of today, in any of its denominational forms, capable of rising to the challenge of such a world and speaking credibly to it? ... My personal answer to this question is that it is not.[3]

The theological case has already been made, but what of the ecclesiological one? The situation of the institutional church (in all of its denominational guises) is at the present time somewhat precarious. All are in a state of uneasy transition from the socially central and powerful position of yesteryear to a future position which seems likely to be a good deal closer to the margins of society, and as Richard Henderson neatly phrases it in his book *The Jealousy of Jonah:* ' ... the choice is between ever-narrowing introversion, and catching a wonderful vision of something new, far greater than anything perceived before.'[4] Throughout almost the whole of the western world at least, numbers are in decline, whether gently or dramatically; but this is a symptom not just of a decline in faith but also of a sea-change in the underlying attitude of contemporary society to the church. Indeed, given that many people seek to nurture a faith outside the institutional church (in anything from house-churches to the New Age movement) and that popular religious publishing is a boom industry at present, it could coherently be argued that this decline in numbers is almost entirely attributable to a change of attitude rather than a loss of faith.

There is undoubtedly a complex web of reasons for this change, but it is our purpose here not so much as to investigate these as to chart their effects. The most widespread of these has been to induce a general spirit of apathy and indifference towards the institutional church – even, as numerous surveys have revealed, among many of those who profess some sort of belief in God, and indeed among those who still count themselves as Christians. The church simply does not touch the lives of these people any longer: its worship fails to engage them and its pronouncements on doctrinal or moral topics simply pass them by. For these people the church is neither a positive nor a negative presence: it has, quite evidently, no presence at all in their lives.

Alongside this apathy there is, among a smaller but steadily growing number of people, an active disaffection with and even hostility to the church. It is likely that this may arise from one of several possible causes. The first of these may well be the perceived inflexible and correspondingly dictatorial attitude of the church. Richard Holloway expresses this frustration particularly succinctly: 'Religion is associated in ... [people's] minds with the imperative mood, with rules and commandments that allegedly come directly from God and must therefore be obeyed without question.'[5] Likewise, I personally know a substantial number of people who see the church as demanding the total acceptance of a non-negotiable doctrinal package and which requires of them obedient submission to its dictates on matters of ethics and lifestyle. And their response to this perception is unequivocal: 'I will not be told exactly what to believe, and I refuse to be treated like a child.'

A second alternative, which will reflect on a particular local congregation as much as upon the church in general, is that it may be felt to be (and often with some justice) too exclusive – something which has the potential to affect many different groups within any given society. Clearly this may emanate from the centre, as has been the case (and sometimes still is) with various groups such as divorcees and homosexuals, but equally a local church may decide to exclude unmarried mothers, black people, or even simply people of a different social class, for example. The dangers of exclusivism are being discovered – and it should be said, in some congregations, addressed – with increasing rapidity in contemporary Ireland as more and more eastern Europeans, Africans, Indians and Chinese come to live among us and create a multi-cultural society.

A third fount of hostility towards the church is the charge that it fails to practice what it preaches, particularly in matters to do with sexuality. Thus here in Ireland immense damage has been done to the Roman Catholic Church especially (and, as is rapidly becoming evident, not only the Roman Catholic Church) by the long series of recent clerical scandals; and in similar fashion the Anglican Church in Canada has encountered sustained hostility from some portions of society (not unreasonably, it must be said) for its complicity and silence on matters related to paedophiliac activity in schools under its aegis.

Between them, apathy and overt hostility are eroding the place of the church in society. This may well turn out to be good for the church in the long run, but it emphatically adds to the need for an altered self-understanding. The church's present ecclesiology was developed in an era when the church enjoyed a very substantial measure of power, prestige and influence (of which ecclesiology more in Chapter One) and it is highly unlikely that such an ecclesiology is any longer appropriate (or even coherent) in an entirely changed set of circumstances. For today the church has no significant power and a much reduced degree of both prestige and influence.

All of this amounts to a compelling pressure from outside for the church to re-think its own identity. At the same time, however, there is an equally implacable pressure from within, a pressure which is generated by the fact that a substantial percentage of even the most devout and committed believers no longer accepts the church's official estimate of itself. So, for example, many churchgoers reserve the right to ignore Roman Catholic teaching on contraception, will openly flout the rules on such matters as intercommunion, or will beg to differ with the church on their understanding of a particular point of doctrine. Among these people there may be relatively few who have articulated just what it is that they are doing but, effectively, what they have done, whether consciously or not, is to begin to do theology in the sort of way advocated by the first two books of this trilogy. They have accorded theology a second order rather than a first order status, and have demanded a degree of *agnosis* in their insistence that there is more than one possible viewpoint on this or that issue.[6]

This trend seems likely to continue as more and more people feel the need to step outside the confines of dusty dogma and find their own space for belief. If this turns out to be the case then the effects are obvious and far reaching. Quite simply, it will not be very long before there is a substantial gap between the church's self-understanding as an institution and the theological and spiritual lives of many, if not ultimately most, of its own members. The church would then be, to use a biblical phrase, 'a house divided against itself', and such a house, as Jesus reminded his hearers, is unlikely to stand for very long.

The possibility – indeed the likelihood – of this widening gap between the church and its own members injects a certain urgency into the task of fashioning a coherent ecclesiology for the church of today. Such an ecclesiology must be consonant with the rest of our theology, and the task of this book therefore is to suggest an ecclesiology which has its roots in a theology of *agnosis*, relationality and new found freedom. To fashion a substantially new ecclesiology is much more than the work of a moment, or even of one book. This book therefore makes no claim to be a fully crafted and definitive ecclesiology, but is rather a series of reflections and pointers which others may wish to pick up and explore. Admittedly the ideas expressed here may turn out to be either more or less useful in helping to generate a functional and coherent ecclesiology for the twenty-first century, but the only certain thing at the present time is that the effort must be made. In a world in which attitudes towards the church (both from within and without) are changing fast, it is almost certain that if the church does not also change then it will either wither into irrelevance or become a fundamentalist prison-house. Neither of these alternatives is attractive, and both must be avoided. This book is one theologian's effort to find, if not perhaps a 'still more excellent way', at least a better way.

CHAPTER ONE

Yesterday's Church

At almost every moment in its two thousand year history, and increasingly so in the last two or three centuries, the church has been in the business of playing 'catch up' in relation to the world around it. Its initial response to scientific discoveries from Galileo and Copernicus to Darwin and beyond has been predominantly negative, and in each case it took many years to even begin to live comfortably in the new world thus revealed. Likewise with a wide spectrum of moral issues. As late as 1938 the Lambeth Conference was still condemning contraception (as the Roman Catholic Church, of course, officially still does), and we have only very recently begun to countenance the re-marriage of divorced persons in church.

In all of these areas the church has found itself time and again to be yesterday's church, but what is happening now is even more far-reaching, in that what is out of date is not merely the church's response to outside events, but the church's whole understanding of itself. It is the church's intrinsic nature, and not just its outward aspect, which is rooted in the past rather than the present.

This is hardly surprising, since almost any organisation is by nature innately conservative, but it will be no easy task to loosen the chains which bind it to that past. Mary Midgely expresses clearly in her memoir *The Owl of Minerva* the almost magnetic force of this pull:

> ... it has surely been a great misfortune for the Christian churches that they have become so centred on the creeds. This emphasis on certain compulsory doctrines came about in early times for political reasons, when various bishops

13

were contending for power and needed clear slogans to distinguish their parties, and it then formed part of the general politicisation that followed on Constantine's acceptance of Christianity as the official religion of the Roman Empire – which was perhaps a real disaster for it. Where religion is used to produce political accord, governments naturally want it to be unanimous, so they are drawn towards heresy-hunting.[1]

If the church's theological roots are so much located in the past, then its ecclesiology (which is so closely bound up with this theology) is equally locked into a bygone era. That this era must be left behind is hardly in doubt, but it must nonetheless be left behind with understanding, and its distinctive characteristics must therefore first be explored a little more closely.

And indeed the place to start is with precisely the governing credal framework whose presence Mary Midgely laments so eloquently. Quite clearly this was not always present, and over the first few centuries of Christian history one can perceive a gradual process of first hardening and then eventual ossification at work as boundaries become ever more closely defined and alternative opinions cease to be options and become heresies.

At the very beginning of the patristic period, the so-called 'sub-apostolic' era, one encounters such figures as St Ignatius of Antioch. At this point in time what is being written is not theological treatises, but largely pastoral epistles much along the lines of St Paul. Much of the content of these letters (to the Romans, Ephesians, Smyrneans etc) is concerned with two things: Ignatius' rejoicing over their faith and the likelihood of his own martyrdom. Admittedly he also refers to the necessity of the unity of the church under the local bishop, but the spirit in which he does so is more redolent of sensitive pastoral advice than of incipient hiero-mania! Doctrines such as the Incarnation and the Trinity are taken for granted – they must have been well enough formulated even by this stage to be immediately recognisable and accepted – but they are not dissected in minute detail or defined too closely or exhaustively. One acquires the im-

pression that there is still substantial leeway for discussion and
even divergence in matters of doctrine.

Skipping over a generation or two, one can see much the same
conceptual freedom at work in the apologists of the mid second
century such as Justin Martyr and, at the same time, and not coin-
cidentally, their self-appointed task is outward rather than inward looking. Thus Justin is simultaneously attempting to do two
things. He is writing an *Apologia* for the Christian faith in an effort
to convince a largely Jewish audience to reckon seriously with the
intellectual and spiritual claims of Christianity, and in the process
he is fashioning a theological language (that of *logos* theology) in
which to do so. What comes across so powerfully in Justin's writings is a sense of the thrill of searching creatively for new ways in
which to speak of the significance of Jesus Christ. Clearly there is
as yet no set language in which to do this, and Justin is entirely
justified in fashioning his own method and vocabulary (even if
borrowed in the first instance from St John). Theological genius is
not yet fettered by ecclesiastical caution and dogmatic jargon, and
this is at least in part because in Justin's writings Christianity is
not so concerned with defining its own identity and excluding
outsiders as with reaching out as eirenically as possible precisely
to those who are currently outside it.

Further on into the patristic period, and certainly in what
might be called its hey-day in the third to fifth centuries, there is
a perceptible and consistent hardening of attitudes. It was in
these centuries that the Christian faith began to be cast in a precise credal form through the pronouncements of the great ecumenical councils such as Nicea and Chalcedon. Likewise it is
these same centuries which have left us with a rich gallery of
condemned heretics: Arius, Apollinarius, Pelagius *et al.* From
this point on the story becomes one of the church exerting an
increasingly firm hold on its doctrinal formulations, and later
on, even its confessional statements such as in the savage to-ing
and fro-ing in England in the mid sixteenth century which re-
sulted in such a large number of martyrs not for the church *per
se*, but for a particular denominational expression of it.

If we move forward to the present day then it is plain that the institutional church (of whatever denomination) still largely sees itself as the guardian of established theological truth. In recent years several Roman Catholic theologians have found themselves on the proscribed list or expelled from teaching posts as a result of expressing views which displeased the hierarchy,[2] and within the Anglican church there are cries of outrage whenever questions are asked concerning supposedly fundamental theological issues such as the Virgin Birth or the resurrection.

Theological control and conformity have certainly been one area in which the church has sought to define itself, but it is equally certainly not the only such area. Thus running alongside this hardening of the theological arteries (and 'oughteries'!) there was a corresponding growth in the sense of the church as a centralised institution. Again this was not present initially and in the first few centuries there was a substantial number of bishoprics each of which was able to claim some sort of primacy: Jerusalem, Constantinople, Rome, Alexandria, Antioch and so on. At most, among these, Rome was accorded the status of *primus inter pares*: it was a primacy of honour and not of power.

Doubtless for the best of reasons, all of this was to change under a succession of popes particularly from Gregory the Great onwards. The claims of other sees to any sort of equality with Rome were summarily dismissed, and the Western church at least came to be firmly anchored to an increasingly powerful Roman centre. Indeed, so dominant did this centre become that in later times it was well able to defy, dictate terms to, and on at least one occasion even demand submission from, the Holy Roman Emperor himself.

Once established this centrally dominated and power orientated structure became the church's characteristic *modus vivendi*. In the Roman Catholic Church this is still (and very clearly) the case today: Rome, with its curia, cardinals and congregations, is still the hub, and it is from Rome that papal encyclicals still emanate in a never-ending stream. Other churches, such as the

Anglican Church, may not be dominated from one centre in quite the same way, but they are often almost equally hierarchical and driven from above. Certainly there may be synods or assemblies through which democracy is proclaimed, but bishops are still powerful beings and wield a degree of influence which extends even beyond that power. In this context it is instructive to note the current degree of unease within the Anglican communion at some of the proposals for greater centralisation and increased collegial episcopal power in the wake of the ongoing crisis over the issue of homosexuality, particularly with regard to the ordained ministry. Specifically, unease has been voiced at proposals to increase the authority of the Lambeth Conference, and especially the rather more frequent Primates' Meeting.

Between them, as they became established, this insistence on control of theology and control of structure bred an increasing degree of self-confidence and even of arrogance in the church's estimate of itself. Initially it was the hardening of theological attitudes which enabled this arrogance to assert itself, for once the boundaries of permissible theology were firmly fixed it was relatively straightforward to decide who was 'in' and who was 'out' and equally straightforward to assure each group of the precise nature of their ultimate destination. It was Cyprian of Carthage who coined the famous (or infamous) slogan, *Extra ecclesiam nulla salus*, but the underlying mind-set had already been there for some time and, at least until very recently, this has always been part of the church's perception of itself.

Once established through the medium of theological control, this arrogance rapidly gained ground in direct proportion to the church's increasing power from about the sixth century onwards. Not only were those outside the church assured of eternal damnation, but they were now fitting objects of coercion (cf St Augustine's Epistle XCIII to his friend Vincentius who had become a Donatist bishop) or, failing that, of destruction, and the church's history is still haunted by the grisly spectres of crusades, persecution of the Jews and the savage suppression of dissenting sects such as the Albigensians.

All of the above features are what might be called internal: that is, they were all generated by the church in response to its own perceived requirements. To these must be added one very substantial external factor which has played an incalculably large role in determining how the church understands itself, and this is the overt connection of the church as institution with the state.

This connection was something which originally very much took the church by surprise. For the first three centuries or so of its existence the church had, indeed, very often found itself in direct opposition to the state, an opposition which had spawned any number of martyrs in the periodic persecutions from Nero to Diocletian and beyond. All of this changed dramatically and irrevocably in 312 at the Battle of the Milvian Bridge. Constantine's vision of a cross was to change the church forever, and one might wish, from Christianity's point of view, that his vision had been of almost anything else rather than a cross. Almost overnight Christianity became the official religion of the Roman Empire and became closely allied to the state: so closely indeed that Emperors could summon church councils, and Augustine (as we have adverted to above) could defend the church's use of the state's power of coercion in the furtherance of its interests.

Since this period, various churches have exploited (and in turn been exploited by) this close alliance with the state. In no particular order these have included (and in three cases out of four still include) the Church of England, the Roman Catholic Church, the Calvinist Church, and a wide variety of continental Lutheran churches. In the case of the Church of England the nature of the connection with the state is overt and enshrined in law: the church is 'established' with all that that entails. The monarch is styled *Fidei Defensor*, the Prime Minister has a major hand in appointing bishops, some of the bishops themselves have seats in the House of Lords, and the church is expected to bless, give thanks, or mourn on behalf of the state at a wide variety of national events. The church is woven into the fabric of national life both geographically and culturally. There is not a square inch of England which is not part of some parish, and even today there are still countless villages where the conjunction of church, cricket pitch and public house forms both the visual and social centre of rural life.

If the Church of England has elevated affiliation to the state to a fine art, then the Roman Catholic Church has gone one better: it has even succeeded in becoming a state! In this respect it actually has much in common with Calvin's Geneva which, for a time at least, was almost a church state. The Vatican has, however, achieved this position *par excellence*. It is at once a self-governing city state with its own bureaucrats, diplomatic corps and bank, and General Headquarters for the world's largest single Christian denomination.

Alongside this 'self-governing' model, a very different one exists (although it is no less closely tied to the state) in the case of several of the continental Lutheran churches. This variety of state affiliation is one in which the church is not exactly subservient to, but yet substantially dependent upon, the state, and it results from the state's beneficent provision of a church tax. Thus, for example, in certain of the Scandinavian countries this tax is levied upon every taxpayer unless they consciously opt out of the scheme. The effect is two-fold. At one level there is an immensely well-staffed and provided-for church: musical standards are excellent and even the smallest parish has its administrator, organist, youth worker and so on. But at another level there is a sense that the state could, in theory, if it so wishes, 'pull the plug' and plunge the church almost instantaneously into chaos.

Whichever model is employed (establishment, city state or financial dependence) however, when it comes to a sense of identity and characteristic mode of being, the effect is much the same. For either way the church has a vested interest in identifying itself with the state, and this will almost inevitably engender a sense of comfort with the *status quo* and a corresponding inflexibility – or at least reluctance – when there is any prospect of change. What is, is comfortable, however outmoded: what might be is unknown and therefore potentially threatening and to be resisted.

All of these factors which we have adduced are, as we have seen, firmly founded in the church's past history, but taken together they have produced – and in large measure continue to produce – one requirement and one practical effect which, I would argue, together constitute the defining features of the church's present self-understanding, even if not of its formal ecclesiology – features which in turn lead to the model of the church which so urgently needs to be amended.

The requirement which this powerful, hierarchical, self-confident and even arrogant church has generated is a demand for a particular cast of mind and mode of behaviour among its members. Complete assent is required to the doctrinal teachings of the church, and unquestioning obedience is required in response to its dictates on morality, liturgy and lifestyle. In former years this was obvious and overt and could be enforced in a variety of ways. There was the threat of direct physical punishment through such instruments as the Inquisition, or more subtly, there was the possibility of legal and civil disadvantage for those who did not conform, as was the case in England until the repeal of the Test and Corporation Acts and the passing of the Catholic Emancipation Act as late as 1829. More recently these penalties have (thankfully) not been available to the church, but the underlying drive towards conformity has not, I think, altered substantially. This is most obvious in the case of the Roman Catholic Church in which the faithful are still reminded, through regular encyclicals, of how the church expects them to behave or what, precisely, they are expected to believe. The same mechanism may not be there in any of the other churches, but there is nonetheless a strong sense, within all of the major denominations, of what the markers are as far as acceptable membership is concerned. The clergy of the Anglican Church (at least in England and Ireland) are still required to subscribe to the *Thirty Nine Articles of Religion*, for example, and everyone is required to have a knowledge of the *Church Catechism* before they are eligible to be confirmed.

At this stage one particular point should be made, and it is a point which will be returned to in greater detail in a later chapter. Thus it may sound as though I am suggesting that a body of church teaching and the imparting of that teaching to church members is *per se* a 'bad thing', and that I am advocating some sot of woolly teaching-less church. Not at all. Clearly the church does have its beliefs and practices, and if the church is to have any kind of identity and internal coherence these do need to be 'common currency' among the members of the church. What I am specifically arguing against is not the presence of a body of teaching, but the absence of *agnosis* and the reification of that teaching, and the consequent attitude which fails to have any room for the concept of a 'loyal opposition' to a point or points of that teaching. And there is here a clear link with the method of theology which I have previously outlined.[3] The church needs to realise – and accept with both head and heart – that its teachings are partial, provisional and open to debate and revision. Even the most venerable statements of the church need to be read by each generation in a spirit of *agnosis*, and faith must have within it a space for creative dissent.

Indeed this change is necessary both from the point of view of theological integrity and also from a sense of self-preservation. Mention was made in the Introduction of a gap opening up between the institutional church and a substantial percentage of its members, and it is doing so directly in response to the church's traditional domineering attitude. That attitude grew up and flourished in an age when society was strictly stratified and most people knew their place to be, however grudgingly, somewhere near the bottom of the heap. Most were ill-, if at all, educated, illiterate and theologically unlearned. All of this has now changed and people feel themselves to be their own masters. Increasing numbers of lay people are theologically literate and articulate, and there is a marked reluctance to be dictated to or pushed around by the church. The frustration of being de-skilled and simply told what to do or believe is powerfully voiced by Angela Hanley:

Whenever I feel like weeping at some of the dictates from the

Vatican, I cherish the little thought that some day, some en-
lightened pontiff might suggest that those who make and
enforce the laws ought to spend, say three months every two
years, wholly *incognito*, divested of all privileges, rank, titles,
pomp and circumstance, living the lives of, and with, those
for whom they make the laws. We might have a very different church indeed. It would be an interesting exercise in
adult formation![4]

From within a different Christian tradition, yet sharing a
similar experience, 'Amen' to that!

If obedience in all things has been the requirement of the
church, then the effect which such a dominant church has had
has been to create what is, effectively, a two-tier membership
and to foster a grossly over-clericalised church. This over-cleric-
alisation has taken three forms which both individually and
cumulatively have effectively reduced lay people to a subservient
and secondary under-class within the church. First, then, for
most of Christian history there have been – to put it bluntly – too
many priests. There is some truth in the old adage that clergy are
like manure: good when spread thinly over the land, but noisome
in an heap! And most of the time the church has had a positive
heap of clergy. There have been many different reasons for this,
even within the confines of Ireland and England: family traditions (one son must be a priest, in Ireland especially), some very
good livings in times of general poverty, a certain job security, a
place in society and so on. But whatever the reason the result has
been the same: a surfeit of clergy, resulting in parishes with
three, four and even five curates until at least very recent times.

Alongside this numerically disproportionate quota of clergy
has run also the esteem in which they have historically been
held. Partly this stems from the societal and educational factors
of a largely illiterate populace referred to previously, but there
has also always been an inexplicable element of mystique about
it. It is almost as if the clergy must never be approached too
closely or made free with, just as the Ark of the Covenant would
unleash dire consequences on those who had the temerity to

touch it! Clergy have, by and large, been placed on a pedestal, and even in today's very changed climate (of outright anti-clericalism in some places) there are still echoes of this around. Most parish clergy still feel themselves to be in the position of needing to decline the pedestal which the parish has ready and waiting for them on their arrival, and in most people's minds there lingers an assumption that the parish house and church are immune from malefactors since it is 'unlucky' to meddle with such holy things. Even the stark realities of the daily parish experience of burglary, vandalism and arson cannot quite dispel the aura which surrounds the clergy, and the general feeling is that even if it happens, it shouldn't happen – and more especially so with clergy than with lay people.

Thirdly, there is the historically all-encompassing scope of the priest's role. This is expressed both in language and in practical matters. The language concerns how a parish is spoken of, and it is significant that in the Anglican Church, for example, a new rector is conferred by the bishop with the cure of souls which is 'both mine and yours'. These words are not in themselves necessarily possessive, and may merely indicate participation in something – as in 'my country', which, unless one is a complete megalomaniac, can only be construed as indicating participation rather than possession. However, in a church sense the 'mine' all too easily becomes possessive, and the priest speaks readily of 'my parish', 'my church' and 'my parishioners' in a way which denotes ownership: a use of 'mine' which is readily reinforced by the various forms of Parson's Freehold which do, effectively, make the parish 'mine'.

In practical terms this all-encompassing scope cashes out in the fact that in the vast majority of parishes it has always been, until well into the last half-century or so, the clergyperson who does almost everything. Clearly there are certain functions which only the priest can fulfil, such as presiding at the Eucharist, pronouncing absolution and giving the blessing; but until very recent times how many parishes have actively welcomed lay visits, lay preaching, lay administration of the sacra-

ments and many other functions which are at least as applicable
to lay people as to ordained ones? Ordination and not baptism
has been elevated into being the primary calling to Christian
ministry. At the same time even the word 'ministry' has been hijacked and confined to those things done by the priest in an
overtly church context: how many lay people (again until the
last generation or so) have had their 'ministry' in business,
school, neighbourhood and so on actively recognised and vali-
dated by the church?

Admittedly all of this is changing to a greater or lesser extent
in almost every denomination as the number of clergy declines,
but even today it is a change which, in many parishes, is being
made under protest as a result of pressure, rather than embraced
willingly as a positive re-appropriation of the rightful ministry
of all the baptised.

What all of the foregoing adds up to is, in effect, a governing
model of the church. This model has not been deliberately chosen
and it is certainly a subconscious and unarticulated one. It is
nonetheless a model of how the church operates (or tries to operate) *de facto* most of the time. It is a model which can be expressed very simply as the 'Dispensing Church', and indeed it is
not altogether unlike the more familiar phrase 'Dispensing
Chemist' with faith and church teaching as the medicine for the
soul. In this model, the church already has all that we need. It
has a clearly defined faith couched in immutable doctrinal statements; it has the right teaching on ethics; it has the sacraments
and its liturgy; and it has (even if in smaller numbers than
heretofore) the 'staff' to dispense all of these treasures. There is
little sense of anyone being able to make any real creative input.
Yes, we speak of people 'giving to' or 'working for' the church,
but this is in very limited and pre-set ways: financial giving,
joining the flower rota, serving on the Parochial Church Council
or Select Vestry or whatever. There is no feeling of a shared endeavour in all of this. For the most part people are expected simply to receive the church's largesse of faith, worship and ethics.

Similarly there is no overt place in this model for partial acceptance of the package – although, of course, it must be admitted that individual congregations may well make room for 'seekers'. Officially, however, the church is, as it were, a package which should be accepted in its entirety, and it is not expected (and certainly not encouraged) that individuals should question, and perhaps even reject, parts of that package.

It is possible that in past centuries this Dispensing Church model might even have been an appropriate one, but it is so no longer. Today it is not only insulting to an increasingly theologically literate church membership, but it is also stultifying and overly restrictive in an age when people both within and without the church are actively seeking spiritually and sincerely wanting to belong to a community which will meet their spiritual needs and countenance their questioning rather than dictate to them. Furthermore, it is patently false to what is actually happening within the lives of both individuals and congregations, a fact which Iris Murdoch pointed out with telling brevity in an interview:

> I feel very close to the Christian church, both Anglican and Catholic, but I can't believe that Christ was God; and a lot of Catholics and Anglicans now quietly dismantle the thing behind the scenes. They somehow agree with themselves that they don't have to take it too literally.[5]

This means that both the task of the church as far as its members and the world around it must change somewhat, and also that its self-identity and self-understanding must change radically. As far as the first of these is concerned, Tom F. Driver has some illuminating hints in a book written as long ago as 1981 and entitled, revealingly, *Christ in a Changing World*:

> ... I am disillusioned with the message I hear from a self-assured Christianity. They declare that the truth is Christ as known in the church and therefore the task of Christians is to 'apply' the truth to the world outside ...
>
> Were the church to take itself more seriously, it would indulge itself more openly in the free play of christic expect-

ation. Liberated from its certainty about Christ past, set free
to improvise in its relation to Christ future, it could return to
the threshold of society open to the creative possibilities of
God. Christ is not a tree of knowledge, to taste whereof is to
gain the knowledge of good and evil. To bring Christ to the
world is not the end we should have in view. Instead, we
should allow a present-future Christ to come to us in the
breaking of bread. The communal body thus formed is in
position to address the world – not in 'truth' but in holy expectation.[6]

Likewise as far as the church's nature and self-understanding are concerned, Marcus Braybrooke posed a telling challenge
for the church in more recent years:

> Another test for the church is how far it can build an accept-
> ing fellowship where people can articulate their own experi-
> ence of God in Christ. This again raises questions about the
> future organisation of the institutional church and whether it
> can or should maintain its present hierarchical structure
> where authority seems to come down from on high.[7]

Between them Driver and Braybrooke point to the need for a
substantially new ecclesiology – and it will also, in the light of
agnosis, have to be one which is aware of its own provisionality
and knows that it in time will need revising. Indeed this is a constant need which Saguna Ramanathan points out in a recent
essay: 'Theology in some sense works against itself; its freezing,
fixing tendency changes that of which it speaks':[8] that is, the living subject matter of theology – God himself – is always in danger
of being frozen into immobility in our minds at least.

Ecclesiology is a branch of theology, and exactly the same is
true here. The church is in danger of becoming frozen by its own
ecclesiology, and this is precisely what has happened to the
Dispensing Church. Any new ecclesiology will need to be fluid,
agnostic and relational, and vitally, not afraid of further change.
A tall order! 'Can these bones live? ... O Lord, thou knowest.'

CHAPTER TWO

The Valley of the Dry Bones

In the previous chapter, having delineated a variety of backward looking characteristics of the church, I suggested that its ecclesiology is substantially governed by the model of a Dispensing Church, and the use of such a model is nothing new. Models have always been valuable tools to assist the church in understanding its own identity. This has been so from the earliest times, for what are St Paul's descriptions of the church as 'a body' or Cyprian's depiction of it as the 'ark of salvation' if they are not models of the church?

The use of models as a primary means of describing the church received in recent years a fresh and vigorous impetus in 1974 with the publication of Avery Dulles' groundbreaking book entitled simply, *Models of the Church*. In this book Dulles put forward a series of five models (Institution, Mystical Communion, Sacrament, Herald and Servant) to help to explain the overall nature of any church. The models could be used singly or in combination, and either way the idea was to assist the church in looking at itself, understanding itself, and setting its priorities or ministry. Dulles was instrumental in promoting the use of models, but his categories are of no direct assistance to us here, since they are largely orientated towards the activities and emphasis of the church rather than towards developing an understanding of its own intrinsic nature as far as its own members are concerned. Thus a Dispensing Church such as I have described could also fit any of Dulles' categories. His models and mine are not mutually exclusive but may co-exist side by side and refer to different aspects of the identity of the church.

Before proceeding to look in more detail at another and more recently proposed set of models, it is worth noting that models come in all shapes and sizes, and they do not necessarily have to be of the intellectually heavyweight variety in order to be illuminating. This was demonstrated to me a couple of years ago by a group of students at the Church of Ireland Theological College in Dublin. I had introduced them to the concept of models as a tool for understanding, and I asked them to attempt to explore their perception of the church through the use of a model. The result was at once entertaining and thought-provoking, and incidentally reflects many of the backward looking, exclusive and restrictive aspects of the church described in Chapter One. The model they came up with was that of an ancient and decrepit bus which ran perpetually round and round the same small route. It never stopped to let anyone get on board, but every now and again it would stop and a few people would be pushed out. Thus the bus became steadily more decrepit and emptier as time went by! This less than flattering picture of the church has impelled me ever since to think that some such project as the present one, designed to look afresh at the identity and ecclesiology of the church, is undoubtedly vital if this *omnibus ecclesia* is to be made roadworthy once more!

Since Dulles' book there have been several efforts to re-think the church in terms of models, one of the most recent and thoughtful of which has been that by the distinguished American theologian, Stanley Hauerwas, in his book, *Resident Aliens*.[1] In the course of it Hauerwas offers various models of the church *vis-à-vis* the society in which it is embedded. He proposes three models of interpretation, which may be labelled, 'Conversionist', 'Activist' and 'Confessional', and they relate respectively to pre-modern, modern and post-modern conceptions of the church. The first picture, the 'Conversionist' model, is broadly similar to the type of church which I have described in Chapter Six of *A Space for Belief*. The modern world is felt to be antipathetic and corrosive to faith, and the church is experienced as a haven from that world. The church refuses to be influenced in any detail, doctrinal or ethical, by the opinions or even discoveries of the world, and faith is seen as something to be maintained in all its purity in the face of the world. The church will tend to close ranks and demand obedience and a strict acceptance of beliefs. Dealings with the world are uni-directional: the church has nothing to receive from the world, but it does have a message to proclaim to it, urging it to turn from its ways, repent and enter into salvation. The church is a kind of Jonah-figure, preaching to the evil city, and indeed one almost imagines that like Jonah this church would also prefer it if the world failed to respond and received its just reward.

This pre-modern response to modernity – although it happens often enough – is a somewhat crude and unreflective one. By contrast the 'Activist' and 'Confessional' models are rather more subtle and involve a substantially greater degree of interaction with the world. The 'Activist' model is a thoroughly modern approach to modernity in which modernity itself is seen as something which is not to be fled from or denied, but embraced and rejoiced in. At its heart is the conviction that the modern world is not a regrettable aberration but a part of God's creative activity, and that even the break down of Christendom is a part of God's providence which is to be welcomed. The past, with its strong and very visible institutional church, will probably be seen as having represented a falling away from the more spiritual values of the early church, and modernity, far from being destructive, is, under God's providence, actually providing the conditions for the church to recover its true but long obscured identity. What is happening, and will continue to happen, is that the church is being called to be less distinctive and less visible and encouraged to dissolve itself in the community in a life of service.

This model may accurately be called an 'Activist' model simply because in these new conditions the characteristic identifying feature of the church will be not its institutional power or its public face, but its activity in the community. For this model, the church is about working with all groups for the good of society: the church will be involved in housing projects, social justice, environmental issues and so on, and it will see these things, rather than overt preaching of the gospel, as constituting its primary mission.

The third model is the response of a church which has entirely accepted the framework of post-modernism. Again (and even more radically) in this 'Confessional' model, the full-blown institutional church has largely passed away. It is acknowledged that post-modern society is a smorgasbord society in which unparalleled numbers of people have an unparalleled access to an equally unparalleled number of choices. They can pick and mix from a vast range of lifestyles, faiths, heroes and gurus. In this climate the uniform monolithic church of the past is of little relevance and less effect. The church's task is to create individual communities which will best nourish Christian discipleship in a world which has such a seemingly inexhaustible range of choices on offer.

This series of models makes a good deal of sense when one looks at the ways in which the church does actually exist in real life. One can see all of these models at work, and the models do serve to enhance our understanding of how different types of churches function. The 'Conversionist' model is alive and well, particularly in the more conservative and evangelical reaches of the church; and from personal experience I know of several parishes where one is required to 'believe as many as six impossible things before breakfast' and where there is a theological time-warp which harks back to the halcyon days of anywhere between fifty and one hundred and fifty years ago. Similarly the 'Activist' model has flourished in many places, from South America with its emphasis on Liberation Theology to the Church of England's 'Bias to the Poor' and 'Faith in the City' initiatives. Admittedly the institutional church has not exactly dissolved in either case, but it has certainly linked itself firmly with the pressing concerns of the wider society rather than confining itself to any narrow ecclesiastical agenda. And even the most radical response to modernity, the 'Confessional' model, has found an echo in the upsurge in the informal 'house church' movement – fellowships of faith which have almost no visible presence in society and certainly no perceptible institutional dimension, but in which the faith of those who choose to belong (and there are many such churches, each with its own unique flavour) may be nurtured in a way which suits those individuals.

So there is much to be gained from a consideration of models such as these, but from our present perspective there are also several problems with Hauerwas' approach and, indeed, every other model-based approach to the church of which I am aware. These problems stem from the fact that none of the models employed is sufficiently all-embracing: all are too limited and focus on one particular aspect of the church rather than on its intrinsic nature. Thus Hauerwas may well be right in identifying his three characteristics, but in the context of the present discussion it is entirely possible for any of these three types of church (precisely as with Dulles' models) to be a Dispensing Church: none of these three models necessitates any major change in the church's intrinsic sense of itself.

In the case of Hauerwas' models, the nature of the limitations is obvious. It is simply the case that none of these models is even attempting to explore the nature of the church *vis-à-vis* its own members, and the question of the church's 'internal' self-understanding is nowhere addressed. Instead what Hauerwas' models do – and do well – is to explore the outward aspects of the church and indicate the different ways in which the church may respond to the challenges of modern society and how it might understand itself in relation to that society.

The second problem with Hauerwas' models (or indeed Dulles', or any others that I have come across) is that they appear to begin from the assumption that the church somehow just 'is'. It is a given entity which may then adjust its activities or its emphases, but the formative nature of that 'is-ness' for everything else about church life is not considered in any depth, if it is even recognised at all. The essential *quidditas* of the church is either largely, or even wholly, ignored. Thus the church always seems to be considered as some sort of pre-existing body to which individuals then come, and the church appears to exist as an institution apart from, and prior to, its own members. And again this helps to explain how the church continues to be, inevitably it seems, a Dispensing Church; for in all of these models there is a parallel between the church and, say, a supermarket. A new supermarket exists before it has any customers: it already 'is' as an entity (including being fully stocked with all of its goods), and customers only then come to it and purchase the goods on offer. So too, it appears, with the church. Somehow the church just exists, and believers then come to it and receive from it. All such models are insufficiently relational, and there is no significant place for any admixture of *agnosis* in the church's theology, since all the church does is to dispense to its members the whole truth which is already known and packaged.

In the face of such partial models, the need is two-fold and a little paradoxical. It is to find a way of modelling the church such that its 'is-ness' is not a pre-judged 'given' but is allowed to come freshly into being, and also to find a model which is broad and encompassing enough to reflect whatever this 'is-ness' or core identity turns out to be.

An appropriate place to start would appear to be with the actual members of the church themselves – just that aspect which is neglected by the majority of models. For if we can establish some distinctive characteristics about the faith lives of individual believers this may in turn enable us to posit certain things of the church of which they are members. What, therefore, is the nature of faith? Undoubtedly in what follows there will be some echoes of ideas expressed in earlier books, but the context is different, and even if the answer supplied now is very similar to that returned previously, there is nonetheless a need to re-state it here for the sake both of clarity and of continuity of argument.

I suspect that for a very large number of people – both believers and non-believers – the word 'faith' conjures up primarily associations of belief. This is hardly surprising when one considers the regularity with which congregations are invited to 'affirm our faith in the words of the creed' – whether Apostles' or

Nicene. These creeds, which set out in detail the Trinitarian structure of belief, are central to almost every act of worship, and assent to them is required at all of the Rites of Initiation – the baptism of children or of adults and confirmation. Furthermore, it is this set of beliefs which is used to define orthodoxy, and failure fully to comply with which leads to the charge of heresy. In the church's apparent understanding of them, these beliefs are primary and are at once the badge of and test of membership.

This is a very convenient approach for the church to take, since it readily defines the bounds of acceptable membership and provides a good yard-stick against which members naturally measure themselves. Expedient and widespread it may be, but is it actually an accurate or justified understanding of faith? I do not think so, for the simple reason that it neither reflects the faith experience of the first disciples, nor even resonates with our own experience of faith as we live it.

As far as the first disciples were concerned (and as I have discussed elsewhere) there was little or no propositional content to their faith. They were not required to confess to any particular beliefs, and their 'rite of initiation' was not the profession of a creed, but a response to the simple summons: 'Follow me.' This pattern was then continued throughout their discipleship. Certainly Jesus used parables to illustrate aspects of the nature of God or the kingdom of heaven, but these are word-pictures not binding statements, and much of Jesus' teaching is concerned with how his followers were to live, and illustrated qualities such as generosity, forgiveness, humility, self-giving and such like. And the effect of these things was such that even after Jesus' death and resurrection these qualities were the hallmark of faith, such that St Paul could organise collections for needy churches, deacons were established to serve the poor and the widows, and the cry could go up from the local populace, later to be recorded as a well-known truism, 'See how these Christians love one another' (Tertullian: *Apologetics* 39).

Mutatis Mutandis the picture is still very similar with regard to our own experience of discipleship. Again it is not primarily

propositional, but relational. As the Indian writer, Stanley J.
Samartha has noted, the biblical understanding of truth is not
'propositional but relational, and is to be sought, not in the isol-
ation of lonely meditation, but in the living, personal confront-
ation between God and man, man and man.'[2] The creeds may be
there, but they are not the heart of the matter. Rather, each of us
has, I presume, some sense of an initial call: a 'Follow me',
whether dramatic like St Paul's on the road to Damascus, or a
slower more gentle urging. And faith is powerfully undergirded
by a sense of response to a person, rather than by an acceptance
of a series of beliefs (although, of course, we may also accept
such beliefs) about that person. Furthermore, just as with the
disciples, our faith is not only initiated but also sustained by its
relational dimension. This is powerfully so when we meet with
the Christ-like qualities of love, compassion and self-giving in
others: there is a sense that Christ himself has been met with,
and our faith is renewed once again. Indeed, this relationality
runs so deep that our awareness of Christ may be rekindled,
when sluggish and dormant, through the commitment of others.
I well remember, for example, early winter mornings when at
theological college in Cuddesdon, when, having walked up the
freezing village street I would arrive in chapel feeling cold,
cross, and distinctly unlike praying. On such occasions the
prayer and joy of others would spiritually thaw me out, and the
activity of worship became meaningful again, and I am certain
that if this was the experience of one ordinand it was the experience of many. Faith is definitely a shared adventure and a
shared journey.

Even more significantly, perhaps, one is regularly brought
up against the sheer depth of love which faith may inspire and
thereby brought in a very real sense face to face with Christ in a
renewed depth of relationship. Again a single example will suffice, an example who impact has stayed vividly with me for over
twenty five years. I well remember in a small South Oxford
parish an elderly lady called Doris. She was an unlikely Christ-
figure (and would have cackled manically if the idea had ever

been suggested to her), with bright red hair and the most squalidly filthy and smelly house I have ever entered. Aged over eighty herself, she had, some years previously, taken in a lodger called Ada. Ada was no relation and no old friend of Doris, but entered the house as a complete stranger. By the time I knew them Ada was well over ninety and senile, and Doris attended to her every need. Doris had endless patience and a total empathy with how Ada's world looked. One one occasion Ada woke in the night, and Doris found her sitting on the stairs convinced that she was on a bus. So Doris sat down beside her and described the scenery they were passing through, until a few minutes later she said to Ada, 'Right, love, here's our stop. Off we get', took Ada by the hand and led her peacefully and happily back to bed! By such actions Christ is daily made incarnate once more, and our faith is fed by being shared in such self-giving love.

There are further implications of the primarily relational nature of faith which properly form part of the subject-matter of the next chapter, but here it is important not so much to deal with these implications, but simply to note the fact of faith's relationality and to realise, therefore, that any satisfactory model of the church must reflect this. The church is not a monolith standing over against its members: rather, it is intrinsically a community of shared faith, experience and story, and this is logically prior to any consideration of the church's role, function or relationship to society when it comes to articulating the church's self-understanding.

From this it follows that the business of ecclesiology needs to begin not so much with *what* the church is, as if it was a body which pre-exists its members, but with *who* the church is, and the nature of the faith of its members will substantially inform the identity of the church itself. In large measure, the church gains its identity from its members rather than *vice versa*, which has all too often been the accepted way of doing ecclesiology.

Ecclesiology done in this manner will not only reflect the relational nature of faith and, as we shall see, be able to accommodate a theology of *agnosis*, but it is also in keeping both with a key insight of the early church, and with the experience of at least one prophetic part of the church today – although it must be acknowledged that this prophetic stance arose in the first instance out of necessity rather than choice.

Looking back to the early church, then, the New Testament makes it quite clear that relationship and community life formed the bedrock of the church's identity. There is not only the familiar passage in Acts 4:32-35 describing the church's communal life, but also the collection for the needy church in Jerusalem (Acts 11:29-30) and the many times in St Paul's epistles on which he either commends a community for its unity or chides and remonstrates with it over its destructive divisions. Later on in the first century a degree of institutionalisation crept in, but the focus was still firmly on the communal life of gathered believers. Thus although, for example, St Ignatius of Antioch has much to say about the bishop being the focal point of the church's life, such that, 'Where the bishop is, there is the church', even Ignatius would have acknowledged that the bishop is not the church all by himself: he is the focal point of unity and authority for a church which is composed of the bishop and all of his fellow believers. The church is primarily a community gathered around the bishop, and only secondarily, if at all, an ontologically separate entity with an identity all of its own.

Just how central this relational identity of the church remains even today – although it has often and for so long been largely obscured – was graphically demonstrated only a couple of years ago by one of the Anglican dioceses in Canada. As with churches of all denominations in various parts of the world, this diocese was suddenly confronted with allegations of paedophilia in its schools some forty or fifty years previously. These accusations led to a substantial number of court cases and the payment of correspondingly vast sums in compensation to the victims. The upshot of this was the immediate threat of diocesan bankruptcy and, if the flood of allegations continued, even the seizure of church property in order to pay off the huge amounts of money involved. In this situation great credit reflected on the diocese, and in particular upon its bishop. There was no attempt to downplay the seriousness of the allegations or the damage done to those who were abused, and equally no attempt was made to escape the consequences of past misdeeds; and the result was the very real possibility that the entire diocese might find itself in liquidation – no property, no stipends, no nothing. One might have expected the voice of despair to echo and re-echo around the church in such a plight. The immediate response of the bishop was, however, anything but despairing, and offers a clue as to a potential and inspiringly prophetic ecclesiology: 'Give us a loaf of bread, a bottle of wine, and a table, and we are in business!'

Here is the church defining itself precisely by its relational gathering in community. Other types of models, helpful though some aspects of them may be, will never succeed in bringing the dry bones of the Dispensing Church to life. It would appear, therefore, to be high time to develop a new relational and *agnosis*-oriented model of the church, and to do ecclesiology from the 'bottom up'. To do this we must return, in the next chapter, to the nature of faith, and explore how the faith of the individual may (and should) shape the faith – and thereby the theology – of the church.

CHAPTER THREE

The Faith of the Church

The distinguished German theologian – and eventually, martyr – Dietrich Bonhoeffer, once said that, 'The Bible knows nothing of solitary religion.' It is in this same spirit that we have argued here that faith is primarily relational rather than propositional, and that this quality of relationality operates on two planes: both 'vertically', as it were, in the relationship which we have with God in Jesus Christ, and 'horizontally' in the relationship which we have with our fellow believers in the life of the church. This relationality is one vital aspect of faith, but there are also others which must be taken into account, and we must therefore now take a closer look at the nature of faith. The following account is not intended to be exhaustive, and there will, from other perspectives than my own, undoubtedly be some omissions. Likewise it is unlikely that any two people will experience faith in exactly the same way, so it may well be that what is said here will not fully reflect the faith of some (possibly many) people. With these reservations, the intent is nevertheless to highlight certain aspects of faith which are crucial as pointers to the identity of the church, and to hope that these aspects are ones which resonate with – or at least produce echoes in – the majority of believers.

First, then, the fact that our faith concerns us with a relationship with God in Christ and with a response to the call, 'Follow me' – and we may recall that the earliest believers were styled followers of 'The Way' and not of 'The System' – means that faith is fully alive to the possibility and value of *agnosis*. *Agnosis* may be anathema to those who would regard faith as a closed system of propositional certainties, but such faith – if it is faith –

is stifling and restrictive, and *agnosis* is very properly a real part of faith when it is creatively and relationally understood. Indeed, a faith not tempered by *agnosis* may even be described as dangerous, as Chris McVey notes in connection with a reflection on Derrida:

> The philosopher, Jacques Derrida, died in October 2004. One who knew him well wrote that in the last decade of his life he became preoccupied with religion and it is in this area that his contribution might well be most significant for our time. He understood that religion is impossible without uncertainty. God can never be known or adequately represented by imperfect human beings. Yet we live in an age when major conflicts are shaped by people who claim to know, for certain, that God is on their side. Derrida reminded us that religion does not always give clear meaning, purpose and certainty by providing secure foundations. To the contrary, the great religious traditions are profoundly disturbing because they call certainty and security into question. Belief not tempered by doubt poses a mortal danger.[1]

In this requirement for *agnosis* in faith, we may, as in so many other things, take our cue from the first disciples. One might imagine that having access to the 'real thing' might have freed them from *agnosis*, yet the pages of the gospels are full of references to their limited understanding and even doubts. For the purposes of illustration we may confine ourselves to three of these, which relate respectively to Jesus' ministry, death and resurrection.

During his ministry there were many times when the disciples failed fully to understand Jesus, but there is perhaps one episode in particular which illustrates the depth of this uncertainty and *agnosis*, even in the midst of their commitment to, and love for him. This is the occasion, recorded in Mark 4:35-41, and reflected in the gospels of St Matthew and St Luke, when Jesus is asleep in a boat with the disciples when a storm blows up on the Sea of Galilee. Even with Jesus in the boat the disciples are terri-

fied and wake Jesus up with the words, 'Teacher, do you not
care if we perish?' At this, Jesus calms the storm, but also,
tellingly, rebukes the disciples: 'Why are you afraid? Have you
no faith?', and the story ends, not in knowledge, but in utter be-
wilderment as the disciples respond in self-evidently mystified
fashion: 'Who then is this, that even wind and sea obey him?'
Even if we wish to dispute (as we well may) the historical accuracy of this account, it still remains true that the early Christian
communities must have entertained the possibility of doubt and
unknowing in order to write or even redact such a story.

If Jesus' life was a puzzle, his death was even more so. Again,
the total historical accuracy of the gospels is not important, since
what they record is either historical fact or (almost as tellingly)
what the early church nonetheless felt to be a justifiable mystific-
ation when writing about the death of Jesus. Thus each of the
synoptic gospels records the disciples' puzzlement and complete lack of comprehension when Jesus predicts his own death
on not one, but three occasions, and indeed, in the case of Peter
this proceeds to an outright rejection of this prediction, for
which he is suitably rebuked. Similarly, it is evident that the significance of Jesus' death as central to his work (which he has
been at such pains to stress to the disciples) never significantly
sank in for them. When that death is imminent they do not, however surreptitiously, attempt to stay near him and somehow witness these crucial scenes: instead, 'they all forsook him and fled'
(Mark 14:50).

The final manifestations of *agnosis* in the gospels are connected with no less a phenomenon than the resurrection. I have discussed in some detail in *A Space for Unknowing* the hesitant and
faltering beginnings of resurrection faith, and there is no need to
rehearse the argument at length here. One detail will suffice,
and that is the revealing comment at the end of St Matthew's
gospel: 'And when they saw him they worshipped him; but
some doubted' (28:17). And what is especially interesting about
this verse is the implication that doubt (which is even stronger
than *agnosis*) and worship are not incompatible. For the sense of

this verse indicates that all of them worshipped even though some of them doubted; and if this were not the case then the verse would read: 'And when they saw him some worshipped him; but some doubted.'

If the disciples could so frequently exhibit *agnosis* and even doubt, then our faith must surely be of a nature to offer us the same latitude. And a primarily relational faith is, indeed, just such a faith. For it is perfectly possible to be following Jesus – to have a living relationship in prayer and worship and a powerful desire to reflect his love, humility, forgiveness and compassion in daily life – whilst having reservations about, or simply being completely uncertain about any or all of the finer points of doctrine concerning his person. So, for example, we may be happy or unhappy, according to temperament or upbringing, with a doctrine such as the Virgin Birth, and there are valid theological reasons for wanting both to affirm and deny it. On the positive side, what the doctrine affirms is the divinity of Jesus; yet at the same time what is achieved by a rejection of it (except as a myth, consciously designed to stress that divinity) is the absolute full humanity of Jesus. For an agnostic faith there is no way of proving the issue one way or the other, and even the biblical writers are not unanimous on the subject. Furthermore this simply does not matter, since it is equally possible (and we cannot fully understand it either way) that Jesus was divine with a human father as it is that he was fully human without a biological human father. What actually matters is not the historical facticity of the doctrine, but the lived experience of and relationship with Jesus himself in which (in whatever ultimately inarticulate fashion) we know him to be both human and divine.

Similarly even with such a central doctrine as the resurrection. It may well be that, faced with this apparently logically impossible phenomenon, we have to suspend judgement as to the precise nature of its happening. Again, it does not actually much matter what form the resurrection took (or for us will turn out to take): what matters is again the experiential and relational truth that Jesus was, and is, still to be known, met, loved and followed. *Agnosis* on propositional matters neither precludes faith nor makes it less strong. A relationally based faith is well-equipped to be passionately committed: it is motivated by the supreme love of Jesus himself, and may even (as in the case of countless martyrs) be prepared to go to extreme lengths in order to witness to the depth of that love; and yet, at the same time, it is well able to sit light to the nit-picking dogmatic detritus which so often encrusts that faith and threatens to substitute dead words for the living Word.

Mention has been made already of the fact that our faith is relational both vertically and horizontally, and if the vertical dimension is receptive to *agnosis*, then that same *agnosis* in turn empowers and refreshes the relationally horizontal dimension of our life of faith. That this is so is simply a function of the openness and inclusiveness of an agnostic faith when contrasted with a rigidly propositional understanding. A faith which consists of known 'certainties' is not disposed to welcome new insights or interpretations. Indeed, almost by definition, it is designed to exclude these and to keep believers on the same (inevitably narrow) path. By contrast, an agnostic faith is fully open to the wisdom and experience of others, and is not afraid to try out new and unfamiliar paths, taking the risk that they may be dead ends for the sake of the possibility of faith's enrichment. As Gerhard Sauter succinctly puts it:

> Dogmatics does not require us to say the last word. What must be said in all circumstances is not the last word by which we stand or fall. We can and should be allowed to make mistakes. We must have the courage to make statements that will need to be revised, the courage not to be prejudiced and block any further advance. This courage frees us from the obligation to get everything right – that is the best experience in dogmatics.[2]

Crucially also, because it has uncertainties and doubts of its own, such a faith is equally accepting of the uncertainties and doubts of others. There is no sense that anyone must be excluded because they cannot accept this or that point of doctrine without qualification. It may well be indeed that this sharing of unknowing and doubt may, far from weakening faith, actually result in a stronger and more living faith as a consequence of its relationality and intellectual and spiritual vitality.

Certainly this was my own experience during my years at theological college. The theological atmosphere might be described by some as corrosive, but it was, both for me and for many of my fellow ordinands, immensely stimulating. It was literally life-giving to come into contact with the fruits of biblical and historical criticism, and to discover that one did not have to attempt to reconcile irreconcilable passages of scripture or assent to the historical veracity of every last unlikely miracle of Jesus. That this study was done in the relational context of common worship was an essential part of the experience: as faith became less propositionally over-defined and certain, so too it became more richly lived and shared as Christ was experienced in community. Lest it be thought that this experience is confined to the rarefied theological hot-house of college, I should add that I have witnessed this same enriching and enlivening of faith through the same combination of *agnosis* and relationship in the more normal and less theologically pressurised environment of parish life.

If the first characteristic of faith was that a relational faith is open to *agnosis*, then the second characteristic as we have just explored it, is equally clear: an agnostic faith is, conversely, a thoroughgoingly relational faith. It is vastly more relational that a purely credal faith could ever be. For an exclusively credal understanding of faith what unites is a set of words, of conceptual beliefs: for faith as we have characterised it, what unites is a shared journey and a shared experience of the God who is at once beyond, within and among us, even if, like the disciples, our worship is sometimes shot through with *agnosis* and doubt.

The third characteristic of faith when it is approached through the twin perspectives of *agnosis* and relationality is that it is never static: it is never something which we have all wrapped up, but rather a realm in which we are ever open to new glimpses and new possibilities and ready to be surprised at every turn by the eternally new creativity of God. This must be fleshed out in theological terms, and we will proceed to this in due course; but by way of illustration this aspect of faith reminds me of the attitude of a ninety-five year old lady whom I met some years ago. When I was foolish enough to ask her what she made of her long life, she administered the sharp and telling rebuke: 'Young man, I have no idea; I haven't finished with it yet!' Not a bad motto for faith, as for life!

More substantially, though, it is both the relationality and agnosticism of faith which impel us forward and prevent faith from being static. At one level, then, our faith is changed and moulded simply because it is open to the faith (and with it the insights and wisdom) of others. An agnostic faith is never locked into its own private world of certainty, but is open to new interpretations and even new doubts. And in this there is a radical new empowerment of parochial lay theology, since it is admitted both that all of us are actually doing theology, and that such theology matters, is valid, and is capable of influencing us.

This shift is vitally important, for again it points to the nature and self-identity of the church as being constituted from within by its members rather than somehow imposed from 'outside', and it also heals the rift between the realms of theology and ordinary Christian living and praying. For a church which operates on a 'Dispensing' model, theology is a realm for specialists: the only theology which can really influence the church is that done by professional academic theologians which the faithful (if, indeed, they are deemed capable of it) are then expected to digest and accept. In contrast to this, a truly empowered lay theology points to a very different model of the church, in which it is fully acknowledged that, at whatever level, all of us are doing theology all the time, and in which the possibly very different theologies do not compete or conflict but mutually inform and enrich.

The result of this (as we shall see more fully when we come to delineate the outlines of a model to replace the Dispensing Church) is a much more fluid and dynamic picture of church membership than is often depicted as being the case. The usual traditional categories of church membership are familiar to many, and almost depressingly so to any clergyperson who has ever been asked to fill in any of the endless series of surveys and questionnaires which seem to emanate from diocesan and national church bodies and university theology departments. The classes of membership may vary somewhat from survey to survey, but they will include categories such as, 'core', 'fringe', 'attenders at festivals', 'occasional attenders', 'marry and bury parishioners' and so on, and inevitably most parishes fall into thinking of people in this kind of way.

These categories are fixed ones, and a parish will observe (joyfully) people moving in towards the centre or (regretfully and possibly reproachfully) people drifting away from that centre. People may move, but the model itself is static – there 'just are' these kinds of status of membership into which people fit. An agnostic and relational faith allows, however, for a much less rigidly defined picture of membership, and these categories become, in a sense, redundant. For an agnostic and relational faith will necessarily be one of oscillation, reacting again and again to its own discoveries and those of others. It will never be still enough to fit neatly into any one fixed category of membership. Thus, if one imagines the common worship, the hierarchy, structures and even the creeds of the church as constituting its 'core', then each of us will drift both towards and away from this core with some regularity. On occasions we will be attracted by its security; on others we will be repelled by its rigidity or over-confidence. We may spend long periods of time either near the ecclesiastical equator or at the poles, but neither we ourselves or the framework for membership is ever static or immutable. Always, for an agnostic and relational faith, there will be movement.

This movement is a function not merely of the horizontal relationality of faith, but also, and perhaps even more powerfully, of its vertical relationality. As we have consistently seen, faith is not primarily defined by articles of belief, but by relationship, and, by definition, a relationship is a living and dynamic entity rather than an unchanging and fixed one. Each of us well knows this in our daily experience of human relationships. Both the relationship and the 'knowledge' which we have of another person will change over time, and there is no possibility of ever reaching a definitive end-point. Thus, for example, I have been married for over twenty-five years, and in that time my relationship with my wife has changed, both as we have changed (and hopefully matured) within ourselves, and as circumstances, such as the arrival of two children, have impinged on our relationship. And one of the great joys of such a relationship is the sense that one never knows everything about another person even in this most intimate of relationships. I am still being surprised after twenty-five years, and I am quite sure that I will still be surprised in another twenty-five years.

The same holds true for our relationship with God in Jesus Christ. At its simplest, there will be times when God seems close to us and times when God is hard to find. More substantially, this dynamic of relationship is one of the reasons why Christians return again and again to scripture: it is apparently inexhaustible, and new insights will suddenly emerge even from passages which we have known all our lives and have read countless times. Also, as with a human relationship, our faith relationship will mature and develop both from within, and in response to circumstances and events in which we discern the presence or the will of God. And, indeed, the only certain thing is that this process is, in this life at least, unending: there is, and always will be, more of God to be glimpsed.

Our relationship with God changes, and this in turn changes us; and this fluidity and dynamic of relationship and change opens up one further tantalising theological possibility. Is God also changed by relationship? Is God in some way (however small) 'different' in the presence of creation, and 'different' again in the presence of sentient humanity? Perhaps even more extraordinarily, is God changed by the new relationships initiated by the Incarnation? Continuing to use the familiar Trinitarian model, are the relationships between Father, Son and Holy Spirit enriched or developed by the Incarnation of the Son? Is the Son, indeed, quite the same Son after the experience of Incarnation? There is a parallel here (although it should not be pushed too far) with the insight of science that any experiment is changed by the presence of an observer. This is not to cast God in the role of 'observer', but simply to suggest that it might be the case that one (and that 'one' includes God) cannot be in any situation without everything, including the 'one' itself, being changed. These questions cannot be pursued here in any depth, but the asking of them is not an abstruse academic irrelevance. For even the possibility of asking such questions militates against the traditional doctrine of the impassibility of God. I have discussed this at some length elsewhere,[3] but the powerful relationality of faith at least suggests that God is, as we are, 'affected' by relationship, and this possibility in turn injects a freshness and a warmth into our side of that relationship, and ensures that there is no possible end-point, since both parties to the relationship are always moving onward.

The fourth and final characteristic of faith as we have approached it here is its relationship with and attitude to the historic credal formulations of the church, which we have already argued are second order rather than first order entities as far as faith is concerned. In view of much of the foregoing material, the question may be asked: does this mean that they are redundant or outmoded forms of expression which ought to be discarded and forgotten? The answer to this is 'No', but an agnostic faith does have a very particular relationship with these historic statements, and would indeed, as we shall see in a later chapter, value certain other things such as story and eucharist more highly than propositional statements when it comes to identifying the criteria around which the church may be said to unite.

This highly ambivalent attitude towards fixed categorical statements is not unique to theology. It is common to many other disciplines also, such as art and philosophy, where for many practitioners, there is a similar reluctance to attempt to fix things in what might be termed 'meta-statements': in other words, statements which make an sort of claim to completeness, certainty or immutability, or which appear to claim any definitive regulatory function for themselves. Peter J. Conradi describes such an attitude particularly cogently in relation to the novelist and philosopher Iris Murdoch:

> Murdoch was not hostile to conceptualising, but argued for a particular, provisional relationship to it …
> … she placed no absolute trust in theory. It should be local and provisional, not general and imperial. It is a means, not an end, and she was as aware as Sartre that most cerebration tries to control experience rather than submit to it. Thought itself tries to freeze what is 'brute and nameless' behind words, to fix what is always 'more and other' than our descriptions of it.[4]

Just so with the credal statements of the church. They are historic expressions of the conceptual content of the Christian faith, but an agnostic and relational faith cannot regard them as absolutely definitive or unconditionally binding. They are, as all such statements must be, 'local and provisional, not general and imperial'. Certainly they are statements to which we will return again and again, but they are open to being complemented by other contemporary formulations. Undoubtedly we will always have the urge to attempt to encapsulate faith in words, which are, after all, the medium through which the vast majority of our mental life is conducted, but each of these attempts, once made, immediately becomes 'frozen', and we are then impelled towards our next equally local and provisional attempt.

These four qualities then, would seem to be the constitutive 'marks' of our faith: it is relational, agnostic, dynamic and provisional. This faith will be expressed in all areas of life, but it is distinctively the faith not merely of individual believers but, as they join together in worship, of the gathered church. As we

have observed earlier, the church is its members gathered together, and therefore the church's self-understanding must reflect its members' understanding of their own faith. The question
must now be addressed, if faith is (or at least is becoming for increasing numbers of people) something approximating to the
account which we have given here, then how might the church
composed of these people best understand itself, and what
model might it use to reflect that understanding? The articulation of such a new model must therefore be our next concern
before we can consider the wider theological implications of
these new and challenging parameters for our contemporary
faith and church.

CHAPTER FOUR

Remodelling the Church

Over the course of the first three chapters of this study I have argued that there is a dominant governing model at work in the institutional church. It may well be that this model is carefully disguised, or is unacknowledged or even denied, but its presence is nonetheless unmistakeable. This is the model which I have characterised as the Dispensing Church, in which the church has an identity of its own 'over against' its own members. The shortcomings – and the deleterious effects on church members – of this model have been pointed out, and a case made that the church's own ecclesiology should be consonant with, and always listening to, the lived experience of the people who together constitute that church.

This being so, we have also had to explore some of the essential characteristics of faith, in the course of which we have been led to a re-estimate of the proper place of conceptual knowledge within faith, arguing that it is of secondary rather than primary importance. The faith thus outlined is distinguished by four 'marks': it is relational, agnostic, dynamic and provisional. These marks of faith are not ones which sit comfortably within the model of the Dispensing Church, and this may explain at least in part why many church members of all denominations regularly feel frustrated by their church – it is one which is all too prone to stifle rather than encourage them.

We have therefore arrived at the point where an entirely new model or metaphor for the church is required, one which will adequately reflect and foster the faith which we have articulated here. As with the Dispensing Church model, any new model will be often unacknowledged, but if taken to heart it will have the potential to transform both how the church sees itself and how it nurtures its own members, as well as how it relates to the world around it and to the experience of other faiths.

Over a period of several years I have been reflecting on what such a model might be, and have tried out the following fledgling model on a variety of gatherings, both lay and ordained. The response makes me all the more convinced of the necessity for some such re-envisioning of the church as is proposed here. The model I have in mind is at once as simple and as thoroughgoing as the Dispensing Church: it is that of a 'Seeking Church'; a church which is, and knows itself to be, *in via*, and which never imagines that it has arrived at a definitive end point.

Just as we have argued for four 'marks' of faith, so too a Seeking Church will have at least four distinguishing features. The first of these is that it will not be a church which claims to have all the answers, but one which will readily acknowledge that there is much that it does not know. This is not the same thing as saying that it will not have a voice or an opinion, but it will be the voice of humility rather than of domination. And this will apply in a variety of areas of church life.

Most obviously this acknowledgement of limitation will operate in the realm of doctrine. Within the kind of faith we have described here, there is plainly room for a wide variety of interpretation on many matters, and a Seeking Church will respect and foster that variety rather than attempt to extinguish it. Thus, with equal scriptural warrant, we may attach much or no importance to the Virgin Birth; we may have radically varying accounts of the atonement; we may differ on our understanding of resurrection; or we may be sceptical about particular pieces of teaching or miracles. A Seeking Church will not brand one view as right and another as wrong, but will provide what I have elsewhere called a 'space for belief' rather than a strait-jacket.

It will apply also not merely in the church's internal affairs but also in its 'foreign policy', that is, its participation in the complexities of ethical and social debate. The tendency of a Dispensing Church is to make up its mind and then to pronounce upon these issues as though it necessarily had the last word to say. A Seeking Church will recognise the sheer difficulty of many of these debates and will listen to those of experience and wisdom without regard to their religious affiliation. Thus the voices of, say, human biologists and doctors will be taken into account amid the minefields of modern medical ethics, and those of local councillors, housing trust employees and so on will be listened to when the church is concerned to contribute to something like an urban renewal programme.

Equally importantly, this readiness to acknowledge incompleteness and limitation will have an effect on individual members and on the different 'sections' of the church. Within the present model it is all too rare for, say, evangelicals and Anglo-Catholics to listen to each other's experience: incense and bells are simply right or wrong according to your point of view, as are preaching bands or full vestments. In a Seeking Church one would hope that such hardened positions would not be drawn up, and that the points at issue would be seen as straightforward preference rather than something approaching moral absolutes. A Seeking Church might even be one where the unedifying spectacle of factional in-fighting was merely an echo in the ecclesiastical memory.

The second mark of a Seeking Church, alongside this limitation of knowledge, would be its acknowledgement of its own provisionality, both in terms of its own being as a church, and in terms of its current stance on any given topic, whether doctrinal or ethical. This would mean that the church would exercise neither a paranoid grip on its own existence nor a stranglehold on any possibility of development or change. Here is perhaps one of the most far-reaching changes which a Seeking Church would involve, and the one which would most radically transform the whole appearance and ambience of the church. At one level this has always been – in principle at least – the ethos of the church. As Stephen Sykes points out: 'All the major European reformers characterised their protest movements as provisional and regrettable necessities, and longed for a time when they would cease to

be so',[1] and indeed, within this perspective Anglicanism in particular has always clearly articulated this sense of its own provisionality: 'All forms of Anglicanism can at best be a contribution to the
Church Catholic, and in themselves only provisional. Nothing is
right merely because it is Anglican.'[2]

In contrast to this excellent-sounding theory, however, the
current ecclesiastical scene, although perhaps less stridently so
than a generation or two ago, is still in practice one of musical
chairs, with different church bodies competing for a shrinking
total membership. Admittedly there are rare and striking exceptions to this, such as the mergers which have produced the
Churches of North and South India, and the union of the
Presbyterian Church and the Congregational Church in England
to form the United Reformed Church. But on the whole the aver-
age church member (and even more so, senior representative)
would be heartily aggrieved if it were suggested that their
church is a temporary phenomenon which might one day cease
to exist as a distinctive entity. By contrast, for a Seeking Church
such a possibility is not a problem: it is indeed a new opportunity.
A Seeking Church contains within itself the potential for change,
since it is not wedded to one fixed position which is conceived of
as definitive. It is therefore open to any change – even the possibility of its own demise – if this is seen to be in the service of a
greater unity or a fuller and less fragmented vision of what it
means to be the church. Indeed, a Seeking Church makes the
chance of such re-unions more likely, since not only will each
church be the more ready to sacrifice its own partial and provisional identity, but also neither church which is party to a union
will be in the business of swallowing the other up. The rich insights, traditions and wisdom of each will be profitably com-
bined, since the Seeking Church has no interest in empire-build-
ing, but only in enriching its communal experience of, and witness to, God. Such a vision is movingly expressed in the hymn
by Richard G. Jones, 'Come, all who look to Christ today', verses
three and four of which read:

Come, young and old from every church,

bring all your treasuries of prayer,
join the dynamic Spirit's search
to press beyond the truths we share.

Bring your tradition's richest store,
your hymns and rites and cherished creeds;
explore our visions, pray for more,
since God delights to meet fresh needs.

At its best, as we have seen in the quotation from Stephen Sykes above, this is how the Anglican Church has thought about itself – as provisional and willing to be dissolved in a greater unity – but one does wonder how this would have cashed out if, at almost any period in its history, the calling to dissolution had materialised. What is needed is for each denomination fully to internalise and live with the truth that its own identity is a means and not an end. It is a means for the nurture of Christian worship and discipleship, and should the time ever come when this can be done with a more catholic and all-embracing means, or with a radically different ecclesial structure, then the provisionality of any particular denomination should enable it to pass away without regret.

This same provisionality would operate not only with regard to the 'being' of the church, but also in its willingness to embrace the possibility of change in any of its stated positions. Clearly the church, if it is to speak coherently, has to have a stance of some sort on major issues, whether of doctrine or of ethics. But this stance is all too often reified and there is no room for development. A Seeking Church will undoubtedly still have a stance (although it will reflect the humility of listening invoked earlier), but it will always be known to be provisional and open to revision. The issues of divorce and homosexuality illustrate respectively how parts of the church at least have embraced a seeking model, and how the dominant Dispensing Church and emergent Seeking Church are currently in conflict.

The topic of divorce highlights just how recent the possibility of any concept of a Seeking Church actually is. Less than sixty

years ago, Resolution 94 of the 1948 Lambeth Conference, a resolution entitled 'The Church's Discipline in Marriage' stated that:
'The Conference affirms that the marriage of one whose former
partner is still living may not be celebrated according to the rites
of the Church, unless it has been established that there exists no
marriage bond recognised by the Church', and this, of course, is
still, effectively, the exact position of the Roman Catholic
Church to this day. Within most of the Christian traditions,
however, a more open approach has developed over the past
few decades, and the re-marriage of divorced persons in church
is now a possibility, even though within the Anglican Church
there is still a requirement for a quasi-penitential service of
preparation. The movement for change has, though, been largely
embraced.

With homosexuality the situation is entirely different, and
the various factions within the church are currently at logger-
heads with one another over the issue. For a small (though one
senses, a growing) part of the church there is a willingness to
consider the re-drawing of ethical boundaries. Thus one diocese
(New Hampshire in the USA) has elected an openly homosexual
bishop, and several churches, most notably some of the Scandinavian Lutheran churches, have elected formally to recognise
homosexual unions and have devised liturgies for this purpose.
For the vast bulk of the church, though, these developments are,
quite literally, anathema.

Obviously there are two ways of seeing this division. From a
staunchly conservative perspective it looks as though part of the
church is abandoning all decency, biblical principles and so on,
and threatening to plunge the whole church into schism. It is,
however, equally possible to view the present position as the
dominant Dispensing Church fighting what history will probably prove to be a rearguard action, against a Seeking Church
which is slowly but surely (and prophetically) emerging. A
Dispensing Church will be slow to countenance any change; a
Seeking Church knows its own provisionality as well as that of
its formulations, dogmas, traditions and even scriptures, and is

therefore open to the potential for new vision and (even radical) change.

That a Seeking Church may be slowly coming to birth even as an undercurrent within the still dominant Dispensing Church was graphically illustrated during Archbishop Alan Harper's Presidential Address to the 2007 Church of Ireland General Synod in Kilkenny. I wonder how many church leaders would have the courage and the vision (and the underlying ecclesiology) to say the following:

> My suggestion is that we take a blank sheet of paper and write on it not what, by accretion, we have inherited from a past generation, but what we now need in order to fulfil the will of Christ in our day.

Powerful, and, from the point of view of a Dispensing Church, dangerous words indeed.

These first two 'marks' of the Seeking Church, in a sense lead logically on towards the remaining two marks. The third 'mark', that of openness, then, is only to be expected from a church which knows its own limitations of knowledge and its own provisionality. A Seeking Church will be one which is open to all, on the straightforward grounds that all are seekers. It will not make demands before membership is conferred, and it will not insist upon even an outward (and even less an inward) assent to a whole package of beliefs. Its model, I suggest, would be the openness of Jesus himself. In the gospels, although he has harsh words for those who come to try to test or trap him, there is no record of Jesus ever turning away anyone who sincerely approached him. People's heartfelt requests were met, and Jesus' only question to certain of these people was the entirely welcoming and open question: 'What do you want me to do for you?' By contrast, the church all too frequently seems to have requirements and expectations, and the result (which I have often encountered in pastoral ministry) is that people are regularly sent away empty-handed by the church because they have not fulfilled these requirements. A common but damaging example of this would be the number of people I have come across who have been refused baptism for their children because they have not been married in church. A Seeking Church would be open to everyone at every stage on their journey of faith and commitment, and it would endeavour to meet the needs of all, however apparently trivial or 'unprofitable' to the church itself.

In doing this, and in not meeting people with the stern face of judgement, the church will undoubtedly sometimes make mistakes, and this possibility, unlikely though it may sound, actually constitutes the fourth 'mark' of a Seeking Church – that it is a church which can afford to be in error. The more a church sees itself as being in the 'Dispensing' mould, the less it can countenance the chance of error, a prime instance of which would be the dogma of papal infallibility which states that in *ex cathedra* pronouncements there is, quite simply, no possibility of error. This may be comfortable, but it is profoundly uncreative, since it closes off for ever the avenue of prophetic risk-taking. A Seeking Church will not assume that it is *de facto* the repository of absolute truth, and will accept that God's will and purpose may be revealed afresh in each generation, and given the *agnosis* of faith, it will also not expect this revelation to be necessarily definitive or unequivocal. The church will therefore be willing to invoke the principle of Gamaliel on numerous occasions and accept that experience of new ideas on ethical or doctrinal stances will manifest the wisdom or mistakenness of these ideas. The church will not assume itself to be always in possession of the truth, but rather in search of the truth in every new situation; and searching, by definition, carries with it in equal measure the possibility either of success or of failure. But, crucially, only if a search is made is there even the possibility of finding anything at all. Otherwise there is only familiarity, and ultimately staleness and sterility.

In these four 'marks' we have outlined, at least briefly, some of the distinctive characteristics of the Seeking Church. It now remains to suggest how such a church is consonant with and faithful to its task as being at once the herald and the manifest-

ation of the kingdom of God. More will be said in Chapter 6
about the theological structure which underpins the model of a
Seeking Church, and here we are concerned only with its task of
pre-figuring God's eschatological kingdom.

What transpires is that a Seeking Church is actually much
better suited as a vehicle for this prefiguring than a Dispensing
Church could ever be. Whatever it may say about itself and its
preparedness for the kingdom, the reality of the Dispensing
Church is that it is too static to be an effective herald of a kingdom which is at once 'now' and 'not yet'. The Dispensing
Church is too firmly anchored in the 'now'. It may talk about the
'not yet' aspect of the kingdom, but there is little possibility of
movement in that, or any other, direction. The Dispensing
Church model is one which, although it may not intend to do so,
actually presents the church as being itself a fixed end point,
rather than being a people *in via*.

By contrast the Seeking Church is just such a body, precisely
because of the various 'marks' which we have outlined here.
Because it is provisional, limited in knowledge, open and so on,
it is not static. It is always on the move, and therefore has the
potential to reflect a kingdom which is both 'now' and 'not yet'.
In its values and in its search for the truth, the church is already
at one level a part of the kingdom; and yet it well knows that
there is more to be revealed, and that the church is not to be rooted
solely in the present, but is always to be looking forward and
moving forward towards the eventual fullness of that kingdom,
the exact nature of which is, and will remain, until it finally
dawns, unknown.

Similarly, just as it reflects a kingdom which is at once 'now'
and 'not yet', so too a Seeking Church reflects the 'hereness' and
'otherness' of God – or in more orthodox theological terms,
God's immanence and transcendence. At one pole God is immanent: he is there to be met with and 'known' in the midst (and
often the muddle) of daily life. God's presence is actively celebrated in worship, and is made manifest in the *caritas* of authen-
tic Christian living. At the same time there is another perspect-

ive at work. The presence of *agnosis* at the heart of the church's faith is a permanent reminder that there is always much more of God than we can grasp, and that for all his immanence God is also profoundly transcendent, beyond all that we can know or say. A Seeking Church therefore has implicit within it the adventure of searching for ever-new glimpses of the eternally self-revealing God whom it worships. This seeking is led and guided by God's immanent presence in the church, and the church (just as with the 'now' and 'not yet' of God's kingdom) is seen to be genuinely *in via*, journeying with the immanence of God towards his transcendence – a journey both with God and to God. This perception is one which is firmly embedded in scripture, as Timothy Kinahan has cogently reminded us:

> In St John's telling of the last supper story, Jesus tells his disciples that the Holy Spirit will 'lead them into all truth'. In other words, Truth is not something which the disciples, at that stage, were in full possession of. Truth was the goal to which the Holy Spirit would gradually lead them. It is almost as though Jesus was promising them a slow-drip revelation, a growth in awareness, a deepening of experience, not a once-for-all flash of illuminating light. He was promising a journey as well as a destination, a journey with God towards God.[3]

A Seeking Church attempts faithfully to reflect what it perceives to be the nature of a God who is at once with us and beyond us.

In its nature, then, a Seeking Church is well-equipped to be a herald of the kingdom and a place of encounter with God. In addition, however, there are perhaps three other positive features of such a church which should be touched upon here. The first of these is that it is a church which is well-placed to relate to the world around it. I have discussed at some length in *A Space for Unknowing* the relationship which theology and faith might have with science and the arts, and a similar relationship holds good for the church as whole and the world in general. Once again a Dispensing Church finds itself at a disadvantage in establishing such a relationship. Whether correctly or not, it is often perceived as making pronouncements about the world with an almost Olympian aloofness. A Seeking Church has no private Olympus from which to make such pronouncements. Knowing its own *agnosis* and provisionality, it is a church which is in permanent conversation with the world around it. And this conversation is a genuine dialogue, rather than the monologue which will tend to be the *modus vivendi* of the Dispensing Church. For a Seeking Church well knows that it has wisdom and insights of its own to offer to the world, but knows also that God's presence and will are not confined to the church, and will therefore be ever ready to receive whatever of goodness, truth and beauty may be proffered by the world. In particular it will gratefully receive the wisdom of science as to the nature of the world, and it will rejoice in the vision of creative artists in every medium as they find new ways to give expression to the things of faith, through which expressions the life of the church itself will be enriched and renewed.

The second feature of a Seeking Church is that it is at once a radically new model and the rediscovery of a very old and long-neglected one. Thus, long ago the Celtic church recognised the nature of faith as a journey, and characterised both the individual Christian and the church as being 'peregrinate': that is, being on a perpetual pilgrimage. Its heroes were those who embarked on long journeys such as Brendan the Navigator and Columba, and the physical journeying was regarded as being a lived-out symbol of the soul's pilgrimage. A Seeking Church is, effectively, a contemporary re-statement of such an understanding, and indeed it is a model which will almost certainly resonate with many individual Christians' understanding of their faith as pilgrimage, given the massive rise in interest in recent years in pilgrimages to Santiago de Compostella, St Patrick's Purgatory, Lourdes and countless other destinations.

In addition to this basic identity as a church *in via*, there is an additional aspect of the Celtic vision of pilgrimage which, if incorporated within the life of today's church, would not only be thoroughly consonant with the concept of a Seeking Church, but would also develop that model even further. This is the notion of each believer having his or her 'place of resurrection' – an idea which perhaps requires a little elucidation before its relevance to the contemporary world can be properly explored. It is perhaps best explained by saying that every individual has a place which is uniquely and especially their own; a place where they feel 'at home' and where the presence of God is felt in a way which is almost qualitatively different from the way in which he is apprehended in any other place. In modern times this sense of a unique place was movingly expressed by the restorer of Iona, George McLeod, who experienced Iona as being a place where there was only the thinnest of veils between earth and heaven. The Celtic attitude was that one of the purposes of pilgrimage was to find this place, and movement and journeying were therefore integral to this search. Finally, if possible, the aim of the *peregrinatio* was to die in this place of resurrection, since one wished to die whilst feeling oneself to be as close to God as possible.

The relevance of this to the Seeking Church is substantial, and depends simply on the re-appropriation of the 'place of resurrection' as a metaphor – as it was also for the Celtic church, since the soul needed to find its metaphorical 'place' just as much as the body might respond to the impact of a physical place. In the context of the nature of the church, it conjures up a model which has greatly relaxed denominational boundaries. The Dispensing Church tends to regard members as 'its own' and guards them jealously, and it is tantamount to apostasy to move from one denomination to another. A Seeking Church, however, will acknowledge the lifelong pilgrimage of each individual, and will recognise that where one begins is not necessarily an index of where one will end on that pilgrimage. Different traditions have different strengths and emphases, and these may well resonate within individual believers at various points during their lives. Thus a Seeking Church will not regard movement as apostasy on the part of the believer or failure on the part of the church, but as a sign of life and as part of a natural cycle of growth and movement as, within the wider church, each individual finds their own particular 'place of resurrection' – a place that may be very far from wherever their journey began.

This possibility of movement within the church, as well as its openness to the world around it, leads on to the final characteristic of the Seeking Church to which it is appropriate to refer here. This is its ability to be at once a very powerfully 'centred' church, which is cohesive and firmly bound together (of which more in the next chapter), and a church which has, in the best sense, no boundaries. A Dispensing Church is clearly bound together, by creeds and a hierarchy and a culture of obedience, and it has definite boundaries. It is safe, if stifling. A Seeking Church will refuse to draw boundaries and is, as we have argued already, open to all, no matter where they may stand on the spectrum of belief. As a result of this openness, a Dispensing Church will level the charge of formlessness at the Seeking Church, and it will therefore be the business of the succeeding chapter firmly to refute such a charge. Openness and coherent identity are compatible.

We have considered in this chapter some of the marks and features which contribute to the openness of a Seeking Church, and we must therefore turn this newly minted coin over and discover on the obverse what, if they are not principally the creeds of a Dispensing Church, are the things which lend coherence and cohesion to this open, provisional and agnostic community.

CHAPTER FIVE

'Bind us together, Lord'

Open, provisional, agnostic ... and formless? Undoubtedly this is how a Seeking Church will appear from within the confines of a traditionally-minded Dispensing Church, and it is true that if the church is so radically to change its own self-understanding, then it will need to develop equally new means of establishing its cohesion and identity in the absence of any continuing total reliance on creeds and dogmas. A Seeking Church will be full of individual believers at very different points on their spiritual journey, and approaching different aspects of their faith with unknowing. Some will be relatively stable and secure in their faith, others may be deeply unsure about some or all of it, and some may simply be hovering near the metaphorical door, watching and listening in an effort to find out what it is all about. In such a church, what is it that might at once respect (and nurture) the unique individuality of each of these members and bind them together in a coherent, meaningful and fulfilling way?

In essence, I suggest that there are three closely related features of the life of a Seeking Church which will achieve this. The first of these – which, as we will see, also forms a common thread running throughout all three features – is the centrality of story. This is an aspect of faith and church which has been substantially re-discovered in recent years by theologians of many different traditions and temperaments, as diverse as, for example, Stanley Hauerwas in America and Kosuke Kayana in South West Asia. Similarly, biblical scholars have re-discovered the importance of the story which lies behind and prior to all discussion of sources, redactions and so on. This widespread re-dis-

covery of the place of story is invaluable to the Seeking Church.
At the heart of it is the renewed realisation that an ongoing story
is, and always has been, at the core of faith.

Indeed, story is at the heart of any community, cultural or
religious, and a community neglects this elemental role of story
at its peril. Richard Kearney is particularly trenchant and astute.
He states categorically that: 'Historical communities are constituted by the stories they recount to themselves and to others,'[1]
and in similar fashion Ben Okri, in his book *A Way of Being Free*,
highlights the importance of story for the presence of any concept of value in a community: 'Stories are the secret reservoir of
values: change the stories individuals and nations live by and
tell themselves, and you change the individuals and nations.'
Kearney, in his study, then continues to relate this specifically to
Christianity, and cites Luke in particular as stressing the 'central
role of narrativity.'[2] Interestingly, he then locates the openness
of any community in its ability to remember, celebrate and re-
tell its narrative origins – just as we are arguing that a Seeking
Church is at once open and bound together by story. He comments that: '... once one recognises that one's identity is funda-
mentally narrative in character, one discovers an ineradicable
openness and indeterminacy at the root of collective memory.'[3]
Conversely (and just as we have argued in connection with the
Dispensing Church) he continues: 'The problem is not that each
society constructs itself as a story but that it forgets that it has
done so. Whenever a nation [or any other community such as a
church] forgets its own narrative origins it becomes
dangerous.'[4] However, it becomes a danger not only to others,
but also to itself, and Kearney's chapter ends with the warning:
'Those who think that they can dispense with historical narrative by *fiat* may ultimately be dispensed with by it.'[5] In those
words are sounded the potential death-knell of a Dispensing
Church.

For Christianity, of course, the story in question begins in the
Bible, and it is no accident that the vast majority of scripture is
cast in the form of narrative. As Paul Ricoeur remarked in dia-

logue with Richard Kearney: 'The important point is that the biblical experience of faith is founded on stories and narratives – the story of the exodus, the crucifixion and resurrection and so on – before it expresses itself in abstract theologies which interpret these foundational narratives ...'[6] For the Jews, this sense of faith as story was self-evident, and it operates in two principal ways. First, there was the straightforward sense that they were conscious of the story as being, in every age, its inheritors and continuers, and the re-working and inter-weaving of this story with present experience is everywhere present in scripture. Aside from the basic story of creation, the story is that of the foundation and nurture of a people, through the patriarchs, Abraham, Isaac and Jacob, and finding a central focus in the deliverance from Egypt and settlement in the Promised Land. Thereafter the story simply unfolds through the creation of Israel, its acquisition of a king, and its triumphs and disappointments among the feuding kingdoms of the ancient near east.

The second operation of story within the Jewish consciousness is a development of this and runs even deeper, and this is the concept that the story is, quite literally, to be re-enacted and re-presented in every generation. This conception is powerfully embedded in such episodes as the quasi-credal framework of Deuteronomy 26 ('My father was a wandering Aramean ...'), and the accounts of the first Passover in Exodus, where it is constantly re-iterated that this is a meal to be observed for all time, and in which the child-parent question and answer format is to keep the meaning of the meal alive for each successive generation. Every Jew, from that day to this, has lived (both as child and adult) the events of Passover, and all, therefore, have not only inherited but vitally entered into the story of that people.

For Christians, too, the experience is similar; we see in the Bible not primarily creeds or dogmas, but a story; the story of the Jewish people which is then fulfilled and (from a Christian perspective) surpassed by the story of Jesus. And it is story. There is no requirement in the pages of scripture to subscribe to particular interpretations or dogmas: there is simply the compelling figure of Jesus, to whom one is invited to respond. And there are stories within the overall story. It is significant that the single most characteristic form of Jesus' teaching is that of parable: a story, easily remembered and vividly illustrating some aspect of God, the kingdom of heaven, or faithful discipleship. Indeed it is highly likely that the vast majority of people, if asked to give one instance of Jesus' teaching, would come up with a favourite parable rather than anything else. Story is at once compelling – we are drawn into it – and endlessly re-visitable: there is always some new aspect to be discovered.

Beyond this simple formulation, though, there is yet one further element in the concept and experience of story which renders it even more enthralling and powerful; and this is the fact that it permanently interacts with the present. Every hearer or reader brings to a story their own feelings, prejudices, hopes, anxieties and experiences, and these will be changed by (and will themselves in turn change) the story.

Leaving the Bible to one side for a moment, the fact that this is so may be readily illustrated by a glance at the realm of children's fairy stories, one of the most enduring and widely read of all story genres. Why is it that every generation responds afresh to Hans Christian Anderson, the Brothers' Grimm and countless other fairy stories? It is not necessarily because they are all great literature, although to be fair, the best of them most certainly are. Rather, it is because there is a small piece of each character within each of us: Hans (an endlessly ironic self-reflexive idea, given that Hans has already, effectively, a small piece of the Snow Queen within himself!), Gerda, Peter Pan, the Wicked Witch, Red Riding Hood *et al*, and this piece responds to and interacts with the ancient story in the present moment.

Just so with the story, and stories, of Jesus. At the level of the general story of the life of Jesus, we can see this interaction of past story with present experience at work in the Sermon on the Mount ('It was said in days of old … but I say to you …'); and in the stories of Jesus we can see it happening as Jesus ever and again challenges current ideas by the telling of a new story which takes up and transcends a current story or interpretation: the Good Samaritan, the stories on forgiveness, the parables of weddings and the kingdom and so on.

But if the story of Jesus interacts with the stories of inherited tradition, so too, and no less so, do our own: and here, of course, that inherited tradition includes the stories of Jesus. And here, most characteristically, the action is a two-way one, as we are moulded and formed by the story which we inherit and, at the same time, have a profound capacity to change that story as it will in turn be passed on to future generations, precisely by our response to it.

Our response to the stories of Jesus is very similar to the response of children to fairy stories. In a strange way we meet ourselves in the parables, and by this meeting are challenged and possibly changed. To take just two of many possible examples, we know ourselves at times to be both the prodigal son and the resentful older brother, and whilst we may occasionally have been the good Samaritan we have also worn the street-crossing shoes of the priest and the levite.

At this level the response, though it may be powerful, is essentially very simple; but the possible layers of our response are almost endless. Perhaps the most multi-faceted form of interaction with our inherited story occurs when we sense that Jesus offers the possibility, through his words or actions, of 're-writing' the story in our own time. This is, I suggest, what is slowly happening over the issue of homosexuality. The story which we have inherited is largely that of outspoken condemnation, and until very recently this has merely been repeated in each new generation. However, we are at last discovering that this could be changed and that there are resources within the story itself which make this possible. Set over against the harsh and largely Old Testament judgements is the outgoing and welcoming love of Jesus himself; and this interacts with our present experience as we seek to discern what constitutes loving and receptive behaviour from one human being to another. Jesus' love for all informs our thoughts, feelings and decisions, such that we may wish to transform the story from one of judgement to one of acceptance.

In all of these different ways, then, the church (both corporately and as individual members), is quarrying and interacting with its rich repository of story: the story of the Bible, of Jesus, and of its own ongoing history. The effect of this is the beginning of the creation of a coherent community united by its shared story, and centred on the life-changing potential of that same ever-changing and developing story. So significant is this element of story that J. L. Houlden can argue that: '... the future lies with ... the narrative mode of belief', and that, 'there is much to be said for just telling the story, letting be, and trusting. So the autonomously human may find a workable and life-giving relationship with the divine.'[7]

If story (and interaction with it) is the first feature of the Seeking Churchs' common identity, then the second such feature is the re-presenting and the making active in the present, of the central and crucial elements of that story, and here there are echoes of the Jewish re-enactment of the Passover to which we have referred previously. Again, Houlden remarks cogently:

> It is not so much that Christian history repeats itself – while there are discernable continuities there has been constant novelty – but rather that in the telling of it the story keeps folding back upon itself.[8]

The place or event where this occurs within Christianity is pre-eminently the Eucharist, in which the church celebrates, remembers and, essentially, re-presents, the pivotal events of the death and resurrection of Jesus.

In many ways the relationship of the church to this definitive and defining act is very similar to its relationship with the more general concept of story: that is, that the celebration of the Eucharist provides both an essential stability and the momentum for change. The stability is obviously provided by the basic unchanging framework of the liturgy: unchanging both in terms of its weekly (or daily) repetition, and its more or less universally common pattern. Such stability is a very powerful force in binding the church together, both across different denominational traditions and across immense geographical and cultural divides. This is demonstrable with regard to denominations simply by the number of people (a movement which I have witnessed for myself) who, as Roman Catholics, for example, have attended an Anglican Eucharist and responded, 'But I felt at home; it is almost exactly the same.' Likewise the consistency of the Eucharist as a cohesive force across cultures and continents was dramatically (and movingly) brought home to me by the appearance of a substantial group of Kenyans in the parish in which I was then working in North-West Donegal. After the first Sunday service which they attended I asked them (naïvely thinking of vibrant 'all-singing-all-dancing' African worship) whether they found our *Book of Common Prayer* service a little dull. 'Oh no', they replied. 'It was exactly what we are used to. We use *The Book of Common Prayer* and *Hymns Ancient and Modern* at home in Kenya.' Several thousand miles away from all that they knew, the familiarity of the Eucharist produced in them an instant feeling of home and belonging. For all their differences, an English rector, a rural Irish population, and a transient collection of Kenyans found themselves bound together by the common experience of the Eucharist.

At one level, then, there is an unshakeable solidity about the Eucharist, in that what is done every time it is celebrated, no matter what the exact form of words may be (although these are often very similar across denominations anyway) is that the life and ministry of Jesus are recalled, his atoning death is re-presented as we 'Do this in remembrance of me', his resurrection is triumphantly proclaimed, as is his risen presence within the church and its worship: 'The Lord is here: His Spirit is with us,' and the congregation is finally sent out into the world to live in the power and love of the risen and ascended Lord: 'Go in peace to love and serve the Lord: In the name of Christ. Amen.'

Within this central cohesive and unchanging event, though, there is equally a tremendous potential for variety and for interaction with the present moment and the experience of individ-

ual worshippers. As far as the form of the liturgy itself is concerned, there is an endless and often dramatic seasonal cycle of
change. At different times of the year the lives of various saints
are commemorated, and emphasis is placed on changing aspects
of the life of Jesus himself, most especially at Christmas,
Epiphany and during the moving procession of events from
Palm Sunday through Holy Week and so on into Good Friday
and finally Easter Day. And these strictly liturgical changes (the
use of Proper Prefaces in the Eucharistic prayer, seasonal read-
ings, the use or omission of the Gloria and so on) are then frequently visually reinforced by liturgical colours, the stripping of
altars, the presence or absence of flowers, and by such symbolic
seasonal practices as the imposition of ashes or the distribution
of palm crosses.

In all of these ways the Eucharist interacts with, and thereby
shapes, the ongoing seasonal cycle of the church's communal
life, but it also interacts with (and changes, and is thereby
changed by) the immediate present experience of the individual
believer: the Eucharist is at once a common (because corporate),
and a profoundly unique (because also individual) experience.
The lived story of the Eucharist is interwoven with the fabric of
the story of each individual believer. At any given celebration of
the Eucharist, where everyone present is overtly involved in the
same event, there will be some present for whom penitence is
uppermost, others who long above all else for the triumphant
praise of the Gloria, and yet others who come bearing a heavy
burden of intercession or personal need. The Eucharist is thereby
'changed' by the experience of the believer, and by the same
token the believer will often be deeply changed by the Eucharist.
Many times I have begun to worship with a heavy heart or a
sense of failure, and been refreshed and renewed by confession
and absolution, for example, such that by the end of the service I
am indeed ready to 'Go in peace to love and serve the Lord.'

In this complex web of stability and infinite variety there is
an evocative and not altogether co-incidental likeness to another
realm of human loving (and the Eucharist is profoundly an ex-

pression of love), that of our most intimate sexual loving. The comparison may at first sound strange, but the resemblance is nonetheless strong. In a long and committed sexual partnership each partner will, over years, come to the act of making love in a huge variety of moods, and may indeed make love for a number of different reasons. Similarly, the experience of making love is at once unchanging and ever different and ever new. Just so with the experience of the Eucharist and with it the experience of God himself, so vividly expressed in the hymn by Sydney Carter:

> You are older than the world can be;
> You are younger than the life in me.
> Ever old and ever new,
> Keep me travelling along with you.

This is at the heart of the church's experience of unity: a common experience of the Eucharist which is both corporate and stable and individual and unique, and which is never static but always moving onward with each new experience.

And vitally, all of this is reinforced by the fact that the Eucharist is not something passive, something which is 'done to' the worshipper, but rather is active, a drama, something which is 'done by' the worshipper. Not only does each person present have a part to play (a role in the drama, if you like), but the liturgy itself has a dynamic, dramatic shape which draws us out of daily life and returns us to it. Thus, after a formal liturgical greeting the service unfolds through the ministry of the word towards its climax in the ministry of the sacrament, following which, with the minimum of delay the congregation is enjoined to, 'Go in peace to love and serve the Lord', and are thereby sent out to live out the thanksgiving and self-offering of the Eucharist in daily life.

By this sending out we are thus led naturally to the third feature of the church's common identity (again connected by the central governing thread of story), which is the church's calling to live out both the story of Jesus and the story of the Eucharist in the *caritas* of its mutual life and in its humble service to the world. Here, once again, as with the central story and the re-presented story of the Eucharist, there is the same unifying dynamic of both stability and ongoing momentum and change. The stability is provided by the straightforward constancy of the calling: the church, in the lives of all of its members, is always to be a community of *caritas* and service. At this level, nothing ever has changed or ever will change. At this point, and with this calling so clearly in mind, it is both interesting and instructive to note just how often and how grossly the church has failed in this calling. And I would argue forcibly that such failure is almost bound to be endemic for as long as the church continues to espouse a predominantly 'Dispensing' rather than a 'Seeking' mentality. For a Dispensing Church will (mistakenly in my view) tend to feel itself to be bound together by visible structures – such things as parish councils, vestries, synods and convocations – and these will all too frequently therefore end up in the foreground and overwhelm the tender shoots of *caritas* and mutual care. When structures come to the fore, then the issues which concern them appear to be of the first order (whether the synod should pass this or that resolution, or whether the parish should support a missionary or replace the roof on the parish hall), and people respond to them as such. The result is that the issues can become divisive, and precisely the structures which are perceived as unifying thereby become the engenderers of dispute and faction. In a Dispensing Church where structure and not *caritas* is the chief instrument of unity, it is hardly surprising that the councils of the church (both great and small) should regularly be the scene of, and catalyst for, some of the most viciously un-Christian behaviour one could ever imagine – the behaviour of some of the Anglican Primates at the present time being a case in point! By contrast a Seeking Church will emphasise, as of first importance, the mutual *caritas* of its members, and this will take precedence over the transaction of business or decisions of policy made through church structures. None of these things is sufficiently important to outweigh the primary calling of *caritas* and service – and it is these, not structures or elected bodies, which will unite the church in its lived story.

At the same time as this fundamental calling imparts a unity to the church, it will also, in a Seeking Church, allow room for difference, development and even change, as the church is, as we have already argued, always agnostic and provisional. And again there is a greater unifying potential here than there is in the more absolute dogmatism of a Dispensing Church. A Dispensing Church will tend to marginalise difference and thus sow the seeds of its own disunity, whereas a Seeking Church will welcome and embrace difference as it endeavours always to find out more about the ever unfolding nature and will of God. What binds its members together is its constant quest, rather than a supposed certainty which may at any moment exclude the waverer or the doctrinally deviant.

We have argued therefore that the Seeking Church is essentially held together by its quarrying of a story, its re-presentation of the central aspects of that story, and its living out of the core values of that story. In the course of this we have hinted at the 'dethronement' of structures and dogmas, and it seems only proper, therefore, to conclude this chapter with a more comprehensive exploration of the place of these things (and especially bishops, or their effective equivalents, and the historic creeds) in the life of a Seeking Church.

From the first it must be acknowledged that it would be folly to suggest that such things either should not or could not exist in a Seeking Church. Structures and creeds have always been there and doubtless always will be, and at some level or another the church does need them. The argument here is that they are present as second order entities and provide a 'form' and a way of working for the church, rather than conferring its basic identity as has often been supposed. Thus church bodies and hierarchies are functional rather than defining. How, then, for example, it may reasonably be asked, does this square with the traditional perception, of the episcopal churches at least, of the bishop as the primary focus of unity for the church in each diocese? In a

Seeking Church has story not usurped the unifying position of
the bishop? The answer to this latter question is, 'No'. Certainly
the reasons why a bishop may be regarded as a focus of unity
will have changed in a Seeking Church, but the position itself
still remains. For a Dispensing Church the function of the bishop
is seen in primarily hierarchical and structural terms, and it is
largely the authority of a bishop which confers the unifying
function. In a Seeking Church, although authority is not abolished, it is seen as secondary, and the bishop becomes the focus
of unity not by reason of power, but because he or she is seen as
the embodiment of commitment to the church's story.

The position is similar with regard to the historic creeds of
the church, in particular the Apostles' and Nicene Creeds. These
are not abolished, but their function is changed. In a Dispensing
Church they are often regarded as the touchstones of faith, setting out what is to be believed and thereby providing an impetus
to unity, or at least conformity. A Seeking Church, by contrast,
will recognise the exclusiveness and possibilities for division involved in such an absolute approach, and it knows itself anyway
to be identified by and united around an ongoing story rather
than by any fixed formulations. In such a church the creeds will
still be valued, but they will slip quietly into a back seat – or perhaps pew: they will not be definitive or defining, but will serve
rather to bring us back to or remind us of various points and aspects of the story. Similarly the creeds will neither govern the
story itself, nor our response to it, nor our continual living out of
that story. Thus we may not all agree with every word of the
creeds, but we agree to say them together because they are inti-
mately connected with the story, and because we wish, by worshipping corporately, to build up the church's stock of *caritas*.

Thus structures, hierarchies and creeds may remain, but they
are no longer the initial primary focus of a Seeking Church. The
identity (and therefore the self-understanding) of such a church
is conferred by its story. The church knows itself to be a community which is gathered around and responding to a story which
is still ongoing, both corporately and individually, and vitally,

therefore, it is a community which both moulds individual lives, and is itself open enough to be in turn shaped by the fresh insights of individual believers. A Seeking Church is at once open, dynamic, and cohesive, and as we shall argue in the following chapter, it not only has a coherent ecclesiological identity but also a substantial measure of theological integrity which is, like the elements of story explored here, both stable enough to undergird it and flexible enough to be creative – for in a Seeking Church both story and theology are, and must be, always ongoing. It is the openendedness of story which makes the Seeking Church a people *in via*, as opposed to a Dispensing Church which can all too easily appear to be a people in aspic! Its theology, as we shall see, must be equally open-ended.

CHAPTER SIX

Theologia Peregrinatii

To date in this volume we have identified the need for a change in our ecclesiology, and explored the defects both of the existing model of the Dispensing Church and of a variety of putative replacement models. In reaction to these defects, we have proposed the alternative model of a Seeking Church, governed by *agnosis*, relationality, provisionality and openness, and we have delineated some of the identifying features of such a church. We have argued that the transition from Dispensing Church to Seeking Church is both necessary and possible, and that the inherited traditional frameworks do not need to be discarded, but rather creatively re-interpreted in order to remain meaningful in the wake of this transition. A Seeking Church has the potential to be at once unified and coherent, as well as open-ended and open-minded.

All of this may be true, but it also needs to be shown that a Seeking Church is consonant not only with ecclesiological, but also wider, more general theological considerations. A church which parts company with its theological tradition is on thin ice indeed and may rapidly cease to be a recognisable part of the Christian landscape. It is therefore the business of this chapter to argue that a Seeking Church is theologically coherent and incorporates a wide variety of theological and spiritual insights in which the inherited tradition, whilst it may be changed, sometimes even radically, is not thereby abandoned.

The journey from theological tradition to theological future may well be an uncomfortable one, since, given the nature of a Seeking Church and the agnostic nature of faith, there will inevitably be a leaving behind of false certainties and an openness to as yet unknown possibilities. But, I suggest, what we will discover is that a Seeking Church is ultimately more faithful in its theology to what we perceive to be the nature of God, as well as to the human experience of faith and prayer, than a Dispensing Church – however impeccably traditionally 'orthodox' its theology may be – is ever capable of being.

First, then, the open, provisional and risk-taking identity of a Seeking Church reflects certain central aspects of our perception of the nature of God and of his activity. Perhaps the most crucial of these aspects is that of the open-ended, risk-taking and vulnerable nature of God. This is a facet of our understanding of God which recedes in direct proportion to the conservatism and traditionalism of the church, and recedes largely, I suspect, precisely because it is uncomfortable and disorientating to live with. It is much cosier simply to espouse a 'God's in his heaven and all's right with the world' outlook (all being 'right' because God is 'in control') than it is to envisage a situation in which God has taken the risk of, effectively, relinquishing control and has placed his omnipotence and omniscience in the hands of a frail and feeble people.

However, the reality – which a Seeking Church is well able to embrace – is that this is exactly what has happened, and one can trace three (and perhaps even four) strands or phases in this divine letting-go. Initially, then, there was the straightforward risk involved in the act of creation, and the fact that this required (if that creation was to be truly free) an act of divine self-limitation. Presumably it might be possible for God to create some sort of a 'self-correcting' universe in which there never could be a natural disaster or whatever, but such a universe would not be truly free and would therefore probably not be ethical: after all, if 'wrong' is not a possibility, what meaning does 'right' have? With this divine self-limitation in mind there is a symbolic parallel here between God's act of creation and that of the creative artist. Any act of creation involves a letting-go on the part of the creator. Once a book, painting, symphony or whatever is completed, it is simply launched into the world, where it may take on an identity which its creator never intended or even imagined. Likewise, its creator has no control over its reception or over anyone's response to it. Inanimate though it may be, the artist's creation becomes, as far as the artist is concerned, a 'free agent' once it leaves his or her hands. So too with God's act of creation: unless we opt for an impossibly interventionist image of God we must assume that the creation is genuinely free to be itself, and that it may develop in ways which were not necessarily intended (although, of course, potentially forseen) by God.

But if the initial act of creation was a risk, how much greater was the risk of imbuing that creation with the potential for the emergence of sentient, self-reflexive beings such as the human race has turned out to be: beings who also have a massive impact for better or worse on the entirety of the rest of their planet? One can sense God's intention in this, as Christian theology has always done: that is, the free response of love to love, but at the same time it is evident that the human race has more than enough potential and ability again and again to frustrate that intention. Again it might have been possible to create a being which inevitably responded to its creator, but would such a pre-programmed response qualify as love? It appears that the whole purpose of God actually depends upon risk, and this may (and more probably should) empower us to be risk-takers also as we seek to respond to the initial risk of God.

But God's risk went even deeper than this, and the letting-go went even further. It went, indeed, as far as Incarnation, of experiencing the life of creation itself. Plainly the degree of risk reckoned to be involved depends upon one's perception of this. For much of conservative, traditional theology there is, effectively, no risk. Jesus just had to be the Christ, and had been so from before all time. Things just unfolded as they were meant to do: the Christ had to be born, live, suffer, die and be resurrected. From the perception of an agnostic faith, however, all of this seems rather too neat and certain and, vitally, it entirely downplays the central feature of Incarnation – the full humanity of Jesus. For *agnosis*, and therefore for a Seeking Church, there is no philosophically necessary connection between Jesus of Nazareth and the Christ. Of this, much more in a future volume, but for the present it is sufficient to insist that it all could have been different. Jesus of Nazareth could have refused or relinquished his vocation to Messiahship: the connection between Jesus and the Christ is not necessary but contingent; contingent upon Jesus' never-ending 'Yes' to God, even in Gethsemane, even *in extremis*. In Incarnation God took the ultimate risk: the risk of failing to become Incarnate, baulked by the free will of one of his own creatures, which God (to be true to himself) would surely no more have overridden in Jesus than in any other individual.

One might think that these three degrees of risk (creation, humanity and Incarnation) would be enough, even for God. But no. For what is God's next move? Having ushered in the beginnings of the kingdom of heaven in Jesus Christ, what does God do next? He leaves the continuation of the whole enterprise in the hands of a deeply flawed collection of human beings, one of whom has just denied him and all of whom have fled in terror at the arrest of Jesus! And so the risk continues, because now the future of the kingdom of heaven is in our hands – equally flawed and often equally ready to deny or to flee in the interests of expediency. A Seeking Church is the only possible response to such a wildly creative and irresponsible deity.

If this sounds blasphemous (which it actually is not), then the way to counter this charge is to turn the whole argument around. What can appear as risk is at the same time the manifestation of an ultimate faith: God's faith in us, and again a Seeking Church using its talents creatively rather than a Dispensing Church holding on grimly to its one talent, is the appropriate response. This idea of God actually having faith in us was graphically brought home to me a while ago by one particular Auxiliary Ministry student at the Church of Ireland Theological College in Dublin. As a part of the 'Creeds' course, the students were asked to write their own contemporary creed. All were good, but one was outstanding, because what emerged (beautifully and movingly 'turning the tables' on traditional creeds) was not a formula expressing our faith in God, but a theological poem expressing God's faith in us. I am very grateful to Katie McAteer for permission to quote this in full:

I am the Lord your maker
I believe in love and life, so I created the entire universe which
is precious to me.
I meet you in creation.
By creating time and space, human history and human freedom,
I formed a special place
where love could be freely returned to me.
I believe in the integrity of creation and its beauty.
I acknowledge that my invitation to love has not always met
with a full response
and so imperfection has crept into my beautiful creation.

I am the Lord your Seeker
born in the normal human way of a Jewish woman called Mary.
Jesus Christ, a real and perfect human being, whose historical life,
mission and message are told in the gospels
by those who knew and recognised me.
I meet you in Christ.
I believe and affirm myself to be the God of love who chose the
human reality of suffering and death as the powerful language
of self-sacrifice
on behalf of others.
I meet you in the grave.
I have given hope to all human kind who should not fear death
because I have shown it to be only a fleeting moment
when life is forever changed, not taken away.
I meet you beyond the grave.
My death and resurrection is an invitation to life everlasting
with me
and a promise that despite death
human beings will also rise and be made whole again.

I am the Lord your Partner

I freely give you of myself so that my love for creation will be
made known
throughout time and space.
I meet you in neighbour and stranger.
I will inspire, comfort and support the fellowship of all those
who believe in me so that they might reject Christian division,
respect Christian diversity and effectively spread the message
of my love across the whole world and throughout all time in
order that all people of every religion and none might believe in
the triumph of my unconditional love over all human imperfection.
I believe in my partnership with you to bring about my new
creation
which will enjoy everlasting life and love with me.
I put my trust in you.
My faith in you will not be misplaced.
To you I entrust my creation and all life.
I meet you in that place I call home.[1]

The only way of doing any sort of justice to this kind of God
is permanently to strive for and seek after the God who has such
faith (more than we ourselves have) in us.

Following closely on from this reflection of the risk-taking
and faith-imbued nature of God, the second theological strength
of a Seeking Church is that it allows for a genuine interaction
with God, both corporately and individually, rather than any
kind of servile and often uncreative 'obedience' such as is demanded by a Dispensing Church where, in fact, the obedience, I
suggest, is primarily to the church and only if this accurately reflects him – which often it does not – to God.

The initial mandate for this partnership relationship is independently given in not one, but both strands of the creation narratives in Genesis, suggesting, therefore, that it is not an ephemeral
notion but one which was firmly embedded at the core of all
Jewish (and later of Christian) thinking. Genesis, as is well-es-
tablished among the world of biblical scholars, contains two
more-or-less independent stories of creation which are at least

partially conflated in the first two chapters of the book. In the first of these two stories, God gives humankind 'dominion' over everything else that has been made: '… fill the earth and subdue it, and have dominion over the fish of the sea and over the birds of the air and over every living thing that moves upon the earth' (1:28). This dominion may have been abused over and again, but the intention of responsible stewardship and partnership with God is evident.

The second story is, if anything, even more remarkable than the first and reveals even more of divine self-limitation and the development of a genuine shared responsibility for creation. One might think that God – as he is represented mythically in the story as doing – having created everything would inform humankind of the names of everything that has been made. Instead, what does God do? 'So out of the ground the Lord God formed every beast of the field and every bird of the air, and brought them to the man to see what he would call them; and whatever the man called every living creature, that was its name' (2:19). God voluntarily hands over the business of naming everything to one of his own creatures, and it should be remembered that names, in the ancient world, were powerful and quasi-mystical things and the bearers of identity. Thus the depth of self-limitation and partnership thus conferred is almost incredible: imagine an artist doing something like rashly leaving a finished novel or painting on a suburban pavement to see whether anyone might pick it up and treasure it, or whether it would be trodden upon or picked up and dumped in a litter bin. And yet this is precisely the risk which God took by immediately turning creation over to other (and, by definition, more fallible) hands.

Interaction and a partnership between humanity and divinity are thus woven into the fabric of creation itself. But they are also intertwined with the story of salvation. This is most clearly attested to in St John's gospel, and given the notorious difficulty, especially in this gospel, of deciding what are and what are not the *ipissima verba* of Jesus, it is necessary to add a word here about the irrelevance of such complete historical accuracy in the present case. Thus in St John's gospel one of two things may be happening and either is acceptable as far as the present argument is concerned. Either St John is quoting the words of Jesus, or else he is placing in Jesus' mouth words which were consonant with how Jesus was perceived by the community of the early church – and which have remained consonant with the church's experience ever since. Jesus may or may not have said the actual words in question, but they reflect the church's original and ongoing experience of genuine partnership with him. The words are these, from Jesus' discourse from chapters fourteen to seventeen of the gospel: 'No longer do I call you servants, for the servant does not know what his master is doing; but I have called you friends, for all that I have heard from my Father I have made known to you.' This experience of friendship and partnership is such that it is the recognised calling of the Christian to be 'as Christ' in the world: to be, in effect, his continuing presence on earth, as recognised in the moving meditation by St Teresa of Avila.[2]

A Seeking Church thus reflects aspects, at least, of our complex (and yet still partial) understanding of God and his activity. We may go further than this, though, and argue coherently that it faithfully echoes each person of the Trinity in turn. We have already alluded to Jesus in the context of partnership with God, but the openness and potential for change in a Seeking Church also resonates authentically with the wider teaching and calling ministry of Jesus, and especially with its characteristic form of the parable which we have explored previously in connection with the idea of faith as story.

Here, though, the crucial element is not so much that of story but the 'function' of the parables – and incidentally a good deal of Jesus' non-parabolic teaching also. Indeed there is a connecting thread of openness and of the pushing back of boundaries and the teasing out of new ideas and attitudes which runs from the parables themselves, through what might be called 'acted parables', through to the calling of certain disciples, and through finally to the lived experience of Jesus himself.

To begin with the parables themselves, there is almost always a boundary-pushing, frame-breaking element in them, and one could profitably explore the parables of the kingdom such as the pearl of great price and the treasure in the field, as well as parables like the Good Samaritan in this light. However, one of the clearest examples of such a process is the parable contained in Matthew 18:21-35, since it is a parable told in direct answer to a question, and which goes infinitely beyond the response which the questioner (Peter) either expected or could even possibly have imagined. The passage reads:

> Then Peter came up and said to him, 'Lord, how often shall my brother sin against me, and I forgive him? As many as seven times?' Jesus said to him, 'I do not say to you seven times, but seventy times seven.'
>
> 'Therefore the kingdom of heaven may be compared to a king who wished to settle accounts with his servants. When he began the reckoning, one was brought to him who owed him ten thousand talents; and as he could not pay, his lord ordered him to be sold, with his wife and children and all that he had, and payment to be made. So the servant fell on his knees, imploring him, "Lord, have patience with me, and I will pay you everything." And out of pity for him the lord of that servant released him and forgave him the debt. But that same servant, as he went out, came upon one of his fellow servants who owed him a hundred denarii; and seizing him by the throat he said, "Pay what you owe." So his fellow servant fell down and besought him, "Have patience with me, and I will pay you." He refused and went and put him in prison till he should pay the debt. When his fellow servants saw what had taken place, they were greatly distressed, and they went and reported to their lord all that had taken place. Then his lord summoned him and said to him, "You wicked servant! I forgave you all that debt because you besought me; and should you not have had mercy on your fellow servant, as I had mercy on you?" And in anger his lord delivered him

to the jailers, till he should pay all his debt. So also my heav-
enly Father will do to every one of you, if you do not forgive
your brother from your heart.'

Asking the question as to how often he is to forgive, Peter is
clearly expecting approbation for suggesting the symbolically
large number of seven times. What he receives is a two-fold
shock: we should forgive to the impossibly large number of sev-
enty times seven, and we should do so however vast the magnitude of the sin against us. One can imagine Peter's eyes widening
in shock and disbelief as Jesus told the parable, and it is equally
only an open and provisional Seeking Church which is ever
going to be fully receptive to the possibility of such huge (and
almost unthinkable) changes in viewpoint as Peter was forced to
assimilate.

This parable is only one of many which might be adduced,
but if Jesus' ability to tell ground-breaking stories is remarkable,
then even more so is his ability to live them in what we have referred to as 'acted parables'. One such example is the story of
Jesus in the house of Simon the Pharisee in Luke 7:36-50, and it is
particularly interesting because it actually contains a genuine
parable illustrating the acted parable:

One of the Pharisees asked him to eat with him, and he went
into the Pharisee's house, and took his place at table. And be-
hold, a woman of the city, who was a sinner, when she
learned that he was at table in the Pharisee's house, brought
an alabaster flask of ointment, and standing behind him at
his feet, weeping, she began to wet his feet with her tears,
and wiped them with the hair of her head, and kissed his
feet, and anointed them with the ointment. Now when the
Pharisee who had invited him saw it, he said to himself, 'If
this man were a prophet, he would have known who and
what sort of woman this is who is touching him, for she is a
sinner.' And Jesus answering said to him, 'Simon, I have
something to say to you.' And he answered, 'What is it,
Teacher?' 'A certain creditor had two debtors; one owed five

hundred denarii, and the other fifty. When they could not pay, he forgave them both. Now which of them will love him more?' Simon answered, 'The one, I suppose, to whom he forgave more.' And he said to him, 'You have judged rightly.' Then turning toward the woman he said to Simon, 'Do you see this woman? I entered your house, you gave me no water for my feet, but she has wet my feet with her tears and wiped them with her hair. You gave me no kiss, but from the time I came in she has not ceased to kiss my feet. You did not anoint my head with oil, but she has anointed my feet with ointment. Therefore I tell you, her sins, which are many, are forgiven, for she loved much; but he who is forgiven little, loves little.' And he said to her, 'Your sins are forgiven.' Then those who were at table with him began to say among themselves, 'Who is this, who even forgives sins?' And he said to the woman, 'Your faith has saved you; go in peace.'

In this episode all of the accepted norms are dramatically reversed: the woman, a 'sinner' has acted better and more lovingly than the Pharisee (a man), and the gravity of a person's sinfulness is linked not to severity of judgement but to the depth of forgiveness and the resultant totality of love. As with Peter, one can imagine Simon and the woman listening with growing horror and burgeoning love respectively as the unlovely become lovely and the unloved become loved. This is a depth of transformation which is, I suspect, not readily available to a Dispensing Church, but only to a seeking one.

So far we have witnessed two levels of inversion or transformation of values in parable and in acted parable. The first is, as it were, more or less external to Jesus – he simply tells a story; the second involves Jesus as an actor in the drama as well as a story teller. Beyond this, however, there are at least two further (and increasingly intimate) levels of personal involvement with this question of values on the part of Jesus which at least imply and at most demand a Seeking Church as the only possible credible response to the second person of the Trinity.

Of these, the first is his choice of disciples. These were to be his co-workers and the people with whom he would form a far reaching (and almost passionate) friendship which would out-last death itself. With this significance attached to the relation-ship, none of the disciples offers an obviously promising possi-bility: a disparate collection of fishermen, zealots, and nonenti-ties. At times, though, there is an element not merely of surprise but also of a total reversal of all expectation involved in his choice of friends. Consider Luke 5:27-32:

> After this he went out, and saw a tax collector, named Levi, sitting at the tax office; and he said to him, 'Follow me.' And he left everything, and rose and followed him.
>
> And Levi made him a great feast in his house; and there was a large company of tax collectors and others sitting at table with them. And the Pharisees and their scribes mur-mured against his disciples, saying, 'Why do you eat and drink with tax collectors and sinners?' And Jesus answered them, 'Those who are well have no need of a physician, but those who are sick. I have not come to call the righteous, but sinners to repentance.'

Levi is not the sort of character whom any self-respecting reli-gious leader would possibly single out as a disciple or co-worker. He is one of the hated class of tax collectors, almost certainly dishonest and on the make, and his guest list for the feast (tax collectors and sinners) indicates that he quite evidently keeps entirely the wrong sort of company. No wonder the Pharisees and the scribes are so scandalised! And yet Jesus points out that it is precisely in this reversal of values and the redeeming of the apparently lost that his mission (and with it that of the dawning of the kingdom of heaven) consists.

The situation is very similar later on in St Luke's gospel (19:1-10) when Jesus calls Zacchaeus down from his tree in order to eat with him. Zacchaeus is at least as disreputable as Levi – he is a chief tax collector – and he has thereby become rich at the ex-pense of others whom he has cheated. This story spells out the mechanics of reversal even more plainly than does the Levi episode. There is the same muttering from the 'righteous', and yet inside Zacchaeus' house the unrighteous becomes truly righteous as he gives away his precious riches and restores four-fold anything of which he has defrauded anyone. The ultimate pushing back of boundaries involved is pointed out by the final words of Jesus: 'For the Son of man came to seek and to save the lost.' Faith and the kingdom of heaven are not about static or legalistic righteousness, but about dynamic change and trans-formation.

A Seeking Church, with its openness and readiness for change and transformation, is therefore faithful to this frame-breaking Jesus in a way which any more static model of the church can never be. Finally, though, and profoundly, a Seeking Church is also true to the risk-taking *agnosis* of Jesus, just as we have argued that it is true to the risk-taking of God. This aspect of Jesus, always there throughout his ministry, becomes increas-ingly evident towards the end of his life and particularly so in his crucifixion. As events move towards their by now seemingly inevitable conclusion, Jesus' state of mind – or more properly, state of spirit – changes. The change comes overtly to the fore in Gethsemane, where St Mark's gospel records that he began to be 'greatly distressed and troubled' (14:33) and told Peter, James and John, 'My soul is very sorrowful, even to death' (14:34).

At one level the reasons for this might not appear very hard to find: Jesus, by this stage, must have known full well what was likely to happen to him, and no-one but a fool would not fear the Roman judicial system and the likely scourging and death by crucifixion. But Jesus' words, while they may encompass a de-gree of natural physical fear, do not primarily speak of this – and indeed the resolve of Jesus never falters, and in his repeated Gethsemane prayer he overcomes whatever fear he may have as he again places himself in God's hands: 'Yet not what I will, but what thou wilt' (14:36). What these earlier words to his disciples speak of is more to do with the spirit than with the body. Knowing what is to happen, Jesus is afflicted at the deepest pos-sible level with a far reaching and soul-searing *agnosis*: he will go on doing what he is called to do, but *agnosis* strips away any comforting certainty of vindication and the internal questions begin: Does this have to be so? Is it the only way? Will it actually be worth all the anguish and agony? Is there truly more here than a gruesome death and a void?

If Gethsemane is the beginning of the opening up of an abyss of unknowing, then in the crucifixion Jesus plunges into the depth of that abyss. Admittedly there are seven Last Words from the cross, but most of them would seem to have been 'written back' into the story in order to square the death of Jesus with other scriptural passages and prophecies. Of these seven, though, St Mark's gospel contains only one, and it is one which has a ring of terrible authenticity about it. It is the searing, heart-rending, despairing cry: 'Eloi, Eloi, lama sabachthani', 'My God, my God, why hast thou forsaken me?' Here in gruesome, humiliating death is the ultimate test, the ultimate risk, and part of Jesus at least dies without knowledge and without hope. A Dispensing Church cannot imagine or encompass this absolute depth of *agnosis*, but in that it is false both to Jesus himself and to other human experience. By contrast a Seeking Church well knows that this sort of *agnosis* is a reality in the soul of many people and in the corporate 'soul' of the church. As individuals and as a church our faith involves us in absolute risk as we live and believe with passionate conviction, but knowing all the time that we could be wrong about all of it. If the one whom we believe to be and worship as the Christ knew the totality of conjoined commitment and *agnosis* then surely his church must do the same.

When we turn to consider the ways in which a Seeking Church might reflect our understanding of the Holy Spirit, the essential point has already been made in Chapter Four in connection with the church's ever moving journey towards the fullness of truth. However, there are three other points which may be made briefly here, two of which suggest that any model of the church should be dynamic and onward-moving, and the third of which speaks of a primarily relational rather than credal content to faith. We may note first, then, the invocation of the Holy Spirit at such key moments in the life of the church (and of the individual), as baptism, confirmation and ordination. This invocation occurs because the Holy Spirit is seen as the one who equips for every new stage of life or ministry. Secondly, and closely related to this, the Holy Spirit is depicted in the New Testament (most notably on several occasions in the epistles of St Paul), as the bestower of spiritual gifts in a more general sense, and these are given not once for all to the church but ever and again to each new generation and to each new believer, and this again suggests that both faith and church have an ongoing and unfolding nature which must be ever open to the new things (and gifts) of God through the Holy Spirit.

Alongside these two elements, and tending in a different direction, there is the regular invocation of the Holy Spirit during the Eucharist, which is mostly done in the context of praying, during the prayer of consecration, for the unity of the church. The implication of this is that unity (as a Seeking Church would obviously hold) has more to do with relationship than with dogma: the church is drawn together and united by relationship in and through the Holy Spirit rather than by any particular form of words.

In this chapter, then, we have explored with some thoroughness the ways in which a Seeking Church will be, in its structures and modes of belief, faithful to and embodying of a number of our convictions as to the nature and activity of God. That it should be so is clearly vital, but at the same time it is equally important that it should be true to – and nurturing of – our own human spiritual experience, and it will therefore be the purpose of the following chapter to indicate at least some of the ways in which this is so.

CHAPTER SEVEN

Experientia Peregrinatii

To date we have been concerned largely with the kind of theological insights – in the strict sense of theology – which are present within a Seeking Church. But every church also has what might more widely be termed an 'applied' or an 'experienced' theology which is reflected or lived out in the lives of those who belong to it. It is these wider considerations which form the substance of this chapter, and it is my intention to indicate that a Seeking Church is excellently placed to respect and nurture this experienced theology – by which term is meant the insights and relational knowledge which each of us brings to our faith, our private prayer and our corporate worship.

The first area in which a Seeking Church can exhibit such nurture is in its acceptance of the experience of doubt, and in its acknowledgement of doubt as a valid component of faith. In the world of a Dispensing Church faith and doubt will usually tend to be viewed as opposites, and one of the purposes of the church is to inculcate the one and eradicate the other: the more firmly and certainly that faith can be held, the better. A Seeking Church works with an entirely different – and, in fact, more biblical – paradigm, as well as one which is more true to how we actually feel about our experience of faith and doubt.

This paradigm is essentially very simple. Far from being opposites, faith and doubt belong together – they are, as we would say, two sides of the same coin – and the opposite of faith is not doubt but certainty. Such a stance is thoroughly biblical as St Paul cogently reminds us: 'For in this hope we were saved. Now hope that is seen is not hope. For who hopes for what he sees?' (Romans 8:24), a sentiment which is echoed by the later author

of the epistle to the Hebrews: 'Now faith is the assurance of
things hoped for, the conviction of things not seen' (11:1). Faith
and certainty are logically incompatible: if we have the latter,
then there is, by definition, no place for the former.

Faith and doubt are, however, natural, if at times slightly uncomfortable bedfellows. They belong together in all sorts of con-
texts, and therefore it is not unnatural to find them side by side
in the life and experience of the church. At a very banal level, for
example, one may have faith in the Arsenal football team and
yet entertain doubt as to whether they can win the Premiership
this season. More deeply, one can have immense faith in a friend
and yet doubt whether they are quite up to the incredibly heavy
demands of a particular job. From the limited point of view of a
Dispensing Church I very much question whether this analogy
would be acceptable, since faith tends to be seen as a watertight
and 'doubt-proof' package which one either does or does not
have. But this is precisely where a Seeking Church begs to differ,
and where the concept of a neat package of faith disappears. We
have already explored the contours of the faith of a Seeking
Church in Chapter 3 and seen that it is open, provisional and relational, and in Chapter 4 that it is centred around a story, and
these things should alert us to the fact of its acceptance of doubt
within a framework of faith. For faith is not a complete package
with no remainder: rather, it is an overall attitude (of confidence,
commitment and so on) which can readily admit of exceptions.
So to return to the second of the above examples, my faith in my
friend is expressive of my total attitudinal response, yet at the
same time this in no way precludes doubts about particular and
specific abilities. Indeed (and this is particularly significant) the
better I know my friend – and therefore the more faith I am likely
to have in him or her – the better placed I am to entertain such
doubts.

The same principles apply to religious faith. A faith which is
centred around relationship and story will never be a monolithic
package. It is perfectly possible to be entirely committed both to
the story and to the relationship and yet to entertain doubts as to

the veracity or necessity of a part, or parts, of that story. We may question, for example, the historical accuracy of the gospels with regard to a variety of miracles; we may be entirely unsure about the birth narratives of St Matthew and St Luke; and we may be sceptical about some of the resurrection stories and the account of Jesus' ascension. Even more deeply than these historically-based doubts, we will almost certainly, at points in our lives, entertain doubts about the presence and activity of God. These doubts will probably say more about us and our state of mind than they do about God, but they are very, and often painfully real nonetheless. And these doubts, however deep they may be, are entirely compatible with an equally deep faith. At this point the significance of the analogy with a friend which I have just used becomes apparent. For just as the better I know someone the better placed I am to doubt something about them, so too the closer one gets to God the more profound, it seems, that doubts become, and the less clearly God is seen. Lest this may seem an improbable claim, we may draw attention to the experience of the mystics – who have already been visited in connection with *agnosis* in volume two of this trilogy. Each of them has their own unique way of expressing this insight, whether it is as a 'Cloud of Unknowing', or St John of the Cross' 'Dark night of the soul', or Meister Eckhardt's 'Nothing'. The words used to describe it may differ, but the experience is recognisibly the same: that the closer we are to God the more our comforting images and imaginings are stripped away, and the more awesome and unknowable God becomes, so that we may begin to doubt whether we have ever really known him and whether there is any possible way of gaining such knowledge. Beyond this soul-searching doubt, the mystics admittedly witness also to an irresistible totality of love, but the darkness and the doubt are firmly enshrined as being at the heart of a passionate faith. Most of us will probably never approach the depth of spirituality of the great mystics, and our 'dark nights' will more probably resemble a 'grey teatime',[1] but on another level the experience of the mystics will resonate with ours, and it is within the openness and *agnosis* of a

Seeking Church that our doubts and dark nights can be assimilated into a rounded picture of an ever evolving and developing
faith. Within a Seeking Church the doubts do not threaten a neat
package of faith – for there is no such package: rather, they are a
part of the unfolding of that faith – they are, if you like, part of its
and our and the church's story.

Secondly, and perhaps even more broadly, a Seeking Church
such as has been described here, is entirely receptive to and consonant with the whole theological enterprise as it has been outlined in the first two books of this trilogy, and with, therefore,
the kind of way in which increasing numbers of people are beginning to approach their theology and their faith. I say 'therefore' because, having shared the ideas contained in those two
books with many different groups of people, both lay and ordained, over several years, the response has almost always been,
'How refreshing. So it is possible to do things in a different way',
and as a result I am convinced that there is a substantial
groundswell of people eagerly looking for a new approach both
to theology and ecclesiology.

I suggest that they are searching for such a new approach for
at least three principal reasons. The first of these is that they
quite simply no longer feel comfortable within a basically conservative and traditionally minded Dispensing Church, and
such discomfort may be either doctrinal or ethical in origin. A
doctrinal discomfort will arise as soon as there is any feeling that
one has, or may be about to, depart from the received norms of
church teaching. Thus, for example, anyone who feels even a degree of sympathy towards the *Myth of God Incarnate*[2] school of
thought or who espouses certain of Bishop David Jenkins' ideas
on the resurrection may well feel that there is no place left for
them within the life of the church. Indeed, the degree of divergence does not have to be anywhere near as extreme as this: I
have witnessed for myself the ramifications (and vilifications)
involved in having the temerity to question the historical veracity
of Jesus' walking on water. And what is so upsetting about such
marginalising or even excluding of the questioner is that com-

pletely unimportant things are made to seem of faith-defining magnitude. I may very well be able to question whether Jesus walked on water or fed 5,000 people on a child's picnic, and, at the same time, still have a fervent belief in the power of his death and resurrection; but the more 'Dispensing' a church becomes, the less such a position is allowable, and the situation ultimately becomes an 'all or nothing', 'take it or leave it' one. No wonder church membership figures continue to fall!

In a similar way, an ethical discomfort will manifest itself whenever scripture, doctrine or tradition (or even all three together) appear to have been applied in an unthinking, slavish or even downright un-Christian way. A prime instance of this would be in the context of the debate about women priests – and more latterly bishops. Most certainly it is true that scripture speaks in uncompromising terms about the position of women in church life, and also that church tradition has almost unfailingly echoed this scriptural voice. However, for a Seeking Church these norms are only ever provisional and there is no intrinsic reason why they cannot be revised. From the perspective of a Seeking Church, a movement towards the 'fullness of truth' would suggest that it is unethical, because unloving and un-Christian, to continue to uphold norms which originated in a far-off, foreign and female-repressing culture, and a believer who thinks like this will inevitably feel increasingly uncomfortable in direct proportion to the traditional-mindedness of a Dispensing Church.

At risk of repetition, but in case it should be argued that the whole issue of women's ordination is 'done and dusted', the same arguments hold true with regard to homosexuality. The Dispensing Church dismisses this as immoral, unnatural or whatever, on the grounds of scripture, doctrine and tradition. A Seeking Church will apply other criteria which allow for the provisionality and reviseability of these things, such as what constitutes genuinely loving and creative behaviour, and whence do we acquire our criteria for judging what is right and what is wrong. The upshot is very simple: a putative member of the Seeking Church will quickly feel very uncomfortable, and probably entirely unwanted, within the confines of a Dispensing Church.

As well as suffering from ecclesiastical discomfort, the second reason why a substantial number of people are currently looking for a new approach to faith, theology and church is that they are coming to faith with huge questions in mind. We have long since left behind the days when one generation succeeded another in the same pew in the local parish church, and when, in a sense, there was no call to think about why one might go to church – one just did. Today there are far fewer 'cradle Christians', and even they are more likely to be questioning of their faith than their forbears were. Ever-increasing numbers of people, however, are approaching the church with either some faint shadowy memories of far-off Sunday School days or, as is even more likely, with no previous connection of any sort with the church. And these people quite naturally come with some very reasonable questions about faith.

One such question, which I have heard voiced more than once, might well be, 'How can Jesus Christ be both human and divine? What does it mean to make an assertion like this, and how can such a union possibly be satisfactorily expressed?' In response to a question such as this, it is not adequate just to be told that this is what must be believed, and that we must simply be content with reciting the creed, 'God from God, Light from Light, Very God of Very God, of one substance with the Father', whether or not we can either understand or precisely assent to what it means. For these people – and quite possibly for many lifelong churchgoers also, if they ever stopped to think about it – the old ways of expressing things no longer work, and the style of church which dispenses them no longer works also, and there is therefore a pressing need for a new theology and with it a new ecclesiology. This need was given acute expression by the Dominican theologian Albert Nolan in a recently published collection of Dominican theology. He wrote about what he called a 'crisis' in theology and in the church, and then commented that

the principle reason for this crisis is that, 'we do not have sufficient bold and prophetic theologians to re-think and re-formul-
ate Christian faith for today and tomorrow.'[3]

These questions to which new answers are required are part
of a more widespread wish, on the part of what I would estimate
to be quite a substantial percentage of Christians, to think more
rigorously about their faith, to learn something of theology and
of biblical criticism, and to find ways of expressing this faith
which are meaningful in contemporary terms. This is not something which a Dispensing Church tends to facilitate: after all, if
you have all the answers, then where is the need for thought or
questioning? This was illustrated some years ago during one of
the periodic debates on the Virgin Birth, when letters on the subject appeared in several English newspapers. One such corre-
spondent – who would not be unrepresentative of a sizeable
constituency of church-goers – wrote: 'What do you mean, do I
believe? What do you mean, what do I think? We don't have to
think about such things, they are given and laid down for us.
They are a part of the few things in life that require no thought at
all. It's a very dangerous question to be asking at all.'[4] The same
picture of an unthinking attitude towards faith was also pithily
expressed by Douglas Adams who commented: 'In England we
seem to have drifted from vague, wishy-washy Anglicanism to
vague, wishy-washy Agnosticism – both of which I think betoken
a desire not to have to think about things too much.'[5] Both Mrs
Bradley and the people about whom Adams is writing are ar-
chetypical products of a traditionally minded Dispensing
Church, and it is small wonder that in such a climate there is a
longing for change on the part of those who may wish to think.

This leads on to the third reason why a Seeking Church represents a desired new approach, which is that it is, as we have
seen, less concerned to present a 'package'. It embraces a theological method which is provisional and which works by
glimpses, metaphors, symbols, images and story. It is a method
which is at once stable and flexible, and which allows for a theology and a church which are well-equipped to interact creatively

with the many other worlds (of philosophy, science, art, ethics and so on) which each of us inevitably inhabits. Precisely because its theology is provisional it is able to indulge in genuine conversation with these worlds, as we have previously argued in 'Two Conversations',[6] and is able also not to be threatened by them. There can be a genuinely symbiotic and mutually enriching relationship between theology and the world (or worlds) around it. In contradistinction to this, a Dispensing Church, to the extent that it refuses these dialogues in favour of a more dictatorial monologue, is always in danger of looking like an ecclesiastical equivalent of the 'Flat Earth Society' which blindly denies the palpable realities of the world around it.

A Seeking Church thus nurtures our applied or experienced theology not only in its acceptance of doubt but also in its willingness to embrace new thoughts, new questions and new approaches. At the beginning of this chapter, though, we mentioned a number of reasons why a Seeking Church is in tune with our own experience, and the third of these is possibly the most significant of all of them: and this is that a Seeking Church is, to put it at its simplest, truer to our experience of prayer (whether corporate or individual), and therefore also of God's activity, than a Dispensing Church is capable of being.

A Seeking Church knows well the mysteriousness of prayer: that it is a complex two-way relationship, the dynamics of which are no more intellectually comprehensible than the dynamics between lovers: that is, there is no way of satisfactorily exploring or explaining precisely how or why it works, or even what we may realistically expect from it, except the reinforcing or deepening of the relationship itself. We have attempted to give some account of prayer in Chapter Three of *A Space for Belief*, but here it is appropriate to expand on this a little, particularly in the light of the account of faith which was elucidated in *A Space for Unknowing*.

That faith was characterised primarily by *agnosis*, and this will therefore form a significant part of our attitude to prayer also. By this I do not mean that there will never be any cognitive or conceptual content to prayer: obviously we will frequently come to prayer with specific needs, petitions, confessions or thanksgivings in mind. Rather, what is meant is that these things do not form the beginning and end of our prayer, and that beyond them there is a realm of totally open two-way relationship between the believer and God. Here is the domain of *agnosis*, in which we simply bring the whole of ourselves before God and wait on him to reveal whatever he will of himself. In this prayer there is no sort of fixed agenda, but rather a quiet waiting upon God. And even in our more cognitive prayers there is still an admixture of *agnosis*, for whilst we may bring our needs or even our desires to God, there is no sense in which we are attempting to tell God what to do, and there is no intent or effort to prejudge what God's response to these prayers should be. It is just the communication of our deepest selves to the one in whose own ineffable self we trust.

This is a model of prayer which is far removed from that espoused by any variety of Dispensing Church, and especially from that which would be favoured by a substantial number of the more charismatically oriented churches. In terms of prayer these tend to operate on a 'Dispensing' model *par excellence*, and will usually teach that God answers prayer in certain very precise ways. And this in turn can lead to some thoroughly pernicious theology, such as the believer being told that when prayer is not answered in the manner requested and expected, it is because they do not have sufficient faith. God becomes a kind of cosmic slot machine: just feed in enough faith and you are bound to hit the jackpot! Even worse than this, though, is the response – which again I have personally come across – that when prayer is not answered in the way requested it is because we are being punished by God.

For most of us, I suggest, these are not realistically the sort of ways in which we approach prayer, and a Seeking Church will stress the essentially relational nature of prayer; and like any relationship we enter it openly and without making detailed stipulations about exactly what we expect to get from it. A Seeking

Church is true to our applied theology of doubt, change and prayer-as-relationship, just as we have seen that it is faithful to our deepest glimpses of the nature of God. The contours of a Seeking Church are thus beginning to take shape, and we must explore next how such an ecclesiology, if once embraced, might transform and enrich the lives of its members, both ordained and, especially, lay.

CHAPTER EIGHT

A Mutual Ministry

Thus far we have largely been concerned to depict how a Seeking Church might appear from the outside: that is, from the perspective of anyone looking at it. We have therefore attempted to describe something of its theology, its self-image and its relationship with the world. In the course of this, something will have emerged about the kind of impact which it is likely to have on its own members, but it is now time to spell this out a little more clearly and in somewhat more detail.

What we have styled as a Dispensing Church is so in two main ways: with regard to the world around it and with regard to its own members, and it is this latter sense which we are most concerned to react to here. Mention has already been made in Chapter One of the almost inevitable clericalisation of a Dispensing Church, but it is important now to explore not just the plain fact that this happens, but also the more significant theological issues which lie behind it, and to arrive thereby at a richer and more empowering theology of ministry than has been the case at almost every point in the church's history.

In what follows I shall be using a number of ideas which first saw the light of day in a paper which I was asked to write as part of a Commission on Ministry presentation to the 2005 Church of Ireland General Synod in Dublin. The reception of this paper highlighted perfectly the difficulty involved in moving from a Dispensing Church to a Seeking Church. After one or two approbatory remarks, I was then taken to task by the bulk of those who spoke. One very senior cleric accused me of being 'un-Anglican', and another berated me for attempting to dismantle the uniqueness of the 'sacred ministry'. The transition may be difficult, and the motives and the method may be misunderstood by some, but I stick to my guns at this point and insist that some such transformation as is described here is neither un-Christian nor un-Anglican, and is essential for the well-being of the church and for the spiritual health and empowerment for ministry of each and every member of that church.

In order to see more clearly what it is that we are moving towards, it is important first to establish what model of ministry it is that we are seeking to move away from. So what, in broad terms, is the ministerial model of a Dispensing Church? In essence, I would suggest, the model on which most of the 'mainline' churches work is one which has been conditioned by both theological and cultural factors. In each case, however, it is the thinking of yesterday which has endured into the present and left us with a model of ministry which is at once outdated and, in the changed circumstances of today, crippling and disempowering as far as the vast majority of church members are concerned.

Theologically, then, our ideas (and our practice) of ministry have been almost exclusively governed by the concept of ordination. To this has been attached a quasi-ontological (and sometimes a full-blown ontological) status, and this has often, whether consciously or unconsciously drawn on the image from the epistle to the Hebrews of being 'a priest for ever after the order of Melchizedek'. As I expressed it in my paper for the General Synod: '... there has often been an aura surrounding ordination and a sense (sometimes spelt out) that after ordination one simply "is" that which one has been ordained to be. It is a "status" and indeed a part of one's "being".' Ordination has been seen in ontological rather than functional terms, and the results, certainly in the present day, are, I would suggest, disastrous.

These results have manifested themselves in two principal ways, one attitudinal and one practical. Attitudinally what has happened (and again referring to my paper) has been 'the placing of ordained ministers on pedestals and a "caste" division in the church between ordained and lay.' This is not perhaps so overt today as it was a generation or two ago, but it is still present, even if more subliminally, and as a parish priest I have spent much of my ministry very carefully dismantling the various pedestals which my parishioners have so kindly and thoughtfully prepared for me.

Practically the result has been, until very recently indeed, the virtual de-barring of lay people from any meaningful participation in the ministry of the church. Perhaps the nearest analogy is that of a medieval monastery with its lay brothers. Yes, they were a part of the monastery, but their function was, effectively, that of servants to the community of 'Fathers': they cooked, washed, dug, planted and so on, while the 'Fathers' attended to the essential business of writing theology, copying scripture and chanting canticles. If they could scrabble together any sort of spirituality in these conditions, like Brother Lawrence, then all well and good. If not, they were still useful. For cooking, washing and digging, read flower-arranging, church-cleaning and serving coffee after the service!

If the theological legacy surrounding ordination is a hangover from a past age, then the cultural baggage which is bound up with it is even more so. And the cultural legacy is also now a patently empty and indeed destructive one as far as both clergy and lay people alike are concerned. What has happened is that for most of Christian history (up until probably the middle of the twentieth century), the pedestal-building tendency of an ontological approach to ordination has been reinforced by cultural factors. Thus those who were educated for ordination were among the relatively few literate, and therefore powerful and looked-up-to, members of society. This may have worked – or simply been inevitable – in past ages, but it is counter-productive today. For the circumstantial differences of education and social standing are now eroded, and ordained minister and people appear in most respects to be equal. But the lingering ideas of 'caste' and 'status' have largely marooned the ordained somehow 'above' lay people and feeling pretty useless: after all, a

modern educated population no longer needs most of the teaching and advice which the ordained person used to be able to
give, since they are quite literate enough to be able to find things
out or work things out for themselves. The system now works in
such a way that the clergy are disempowered by the laity and
vice versa.

The final upshot of this mixtum-gatherum of theology and
culture is a predominantly theological mistake: that the primary
calling to ministry is identified as that of ordination and not baptism. Ministry is what is seen as being 'done' by the ordained to
the non-ordained, hence the internal (as well, as we have seen,
external) identity of a Dispensing Church. Indeed, in this connection it is no accident that the terms 'ministry' and 'vocation'
have been, for centuries, completely hijacked by those in collars.
Lay people evidently have no business with such important and
far-reaching things.

For a Seeking Church, all of this is almost entirely reversed,
and the results, depending upon one's perspective, are either
life-preserving or almost unthinkable! There are, in essence,
three major and closely related changes which such a church
will make in its understanding of ministry. First, as one's answer
to this question will govern everything else, there is the issue of
what one identifies as the primary calling to, and empowerment
for ministry. For a Dispensing Church, as we have seen, the answer to this is ordination, and ministry is largely that which is
done by the ordained. Within a Seeking Church, however, there
is a very different understanding both of ministry and, as we
shall see in a moment, of ordination, and the primary calling to
ministry is seen as that of baptism. This is what incorporates us
as members into Christ's church, and in that membership we are
both called and empowered to a life of service and love – and
these things are the very heart of Christian ministry. All of the
baptised are Christian ministers, exercising different functions
and gifts within the whole Body of Christ.

This mention of functions and gifts leads us on naturally to
the second change which will be made by a Seeking Church, and

this is its way of understanding ordination. The change can be
very simply expressed – although it will need to be teased out a
little – as being a change of perspective from ontology to function. We have seen that for a Dispensing Church ordination confers a special 'quality', and that the ordained person just 'is' a
priest: ordination bestows a unique and indelible ontological
status. For a Seeking Church this is no longer so. Any ontological change has been conferred already by baptism and incorpor-
ation into the Body of Christ, and after this point all further
distinctions are functional rather than ontological. Certainly the
ordained person has a different (and very specific) function
within the church from that of a lay person – and we will look
more closely at this in due course – but ordained and lay are not
different kinds or orders of being. To a Dispensing Church this
may well sound like heresy – as I discovered at the Church of
Ireland General Synod – but in fact it takes cognisance of three
often neglected aspects of ordained ministry which are actually
embedded in liturgy and Canon Law, even if, in the interests of
ontological hyperbole, a Dispensing Church usually chooses to
ignore them.

The first of these is that one is, quite simply, ordained,
whether as deacon, priest or bishop, not to *be* but to *do* certain
things. There is little point in citing each of the services of ordination, but each contains a section setting out the duties of those
to be ordained. Thus the Church of Ireland's service for the ordination of priests (which would be more or less reflected in any
church which ordains to the priesthood) reads:

> Priests (or presbyters) in the Church of God are called to
> work with the bishop and with other priests as servants and
> shepherds among the people to whom they are sent.
> They are to proclaim the Word of the Lord, to call those who
> hear to repentance, and in Christ's name to pronounce absol-
> ution and declare the forgiveness of sins.
> They are to baptize, and to catechize.
> They are to preside at the celebration of the Holy Communion.

They are to lead God's people in prayer and worship, to intercede for them, to bless them in the name of the Lord, and to teach and encourage them by word and example.

They are to minister to the sick and to prepare the dying for their death.

They must always set the Good Shepherd before them as the pattern of their calling, caring for the people committed to their charge, and joining with them in a common witness, that the world may come to know God's glory and love.

Similarly, the appropriate duties are laid out for deacons and bishops in their respective ordination services.

Following on from this flows the second neglected aspect of ordination, which is that, certainly within the Anglican Communion, one cannot be ordained *in vaccuo*. Ordination is always, and without exception, to a specific place and role. Both deacons and priests are ordained to work initially in a particular parish, and bishops – with the possible exception of Provincial Episcopal Visitors, or 'flying bishops', who are anyway an extreme form of logical and ecclesiological nonsense – are always consecrated to be the bishop of a specific geographical area. As I expressed it somewhat tersely in my synod paper: 'Ordained is what ordained does!'

The third aspect of ordination which is neglected by an ontological approach and recovered by a more functional one is the realisation that ordination is not indelible, and again I refer to the arguments as originally expressed in my paper:

Ordination confers the right to function as an ordained minister. Thus one can, by retirement or resignation, forfeit this right to function until it is next conferred by a subsequent institution, licensing or whatever. In the meantime one only has the potential to function as an ordained minister – which is what ordination conveys: the right to function *as*, not the ontology to *be*.

A Seeking Church will thus have a radically different understanding of ordained ministry from that of a Dispensing Church, but it is one which is empowering both for clergy and lay people alike, and also faithful to a central New Testament insight about the nature of ministry which tends to be obscured by our use of the word 'priest'. This insight must now be briefly addressed before we can then proceed to explore further the implications and character of the ministry of a Seeking Church.

What may be conveniently forgotten in discussions of priesthood, then, is that our word 'priest' is used to translate two different Greek words in the New Testament, and each of these words has very specific overtones. One of these words, *presbuteros*, signifies a straightforwardly functional role of leadership within the church. It may be used either in the slightly loose sense of the kind of wise, senior person to whom others turn naturally for advice, or – and more frequently – it may be used to signify a person specifically identified and authorised to exercise leadership. This is the kind of function which a Seeking Church would understand as being that of the ordained minister.

However, in the mind of a Dispensing Church, this usage is usually conflated with at least echoes of the other New Testament word in question, *hiereus*. This word is specifically religious and cultic and does have ontological overtones, and it refers to the person appointed to offer sacrifice on behalf of the community and to act as a mediator between the community and God. What a Seeking Church will remember, however, and what a Dispensing Church may well try to gloss over, is that this word is only ever applied to Jesus in the New Testament, and never to any of the leaders of the emerging church.

The implications of this for ministry are huge. There is only one Priest (*Hiereus*), Jesus Christ, and the religious, cultic, quasi-ontological priest is no longer necessary. But, however, and again completely in keeping with New Testament usage, there may be only one *Hiereus*, but there is a corporate *Hierosune* (priesthood) which every baptised member of the church shares in by virtue of being incorporated into the Body of Christ, the only *Hiereus*. In this sense every Christian, ordained or lay, shares in this 'priesthood of all believers', and within this new correctly defined priesthood, everything again comes down to function as different people exercise different gifts and take up different roles, whether of leadership, teaching, administration or whatever.

So what, ultimately, are the implications for ministry of all this? Essentially the single most significant thing is that the role of presbyter (what we so often casually call 'priest') is much narrower than is often supposed, and the role of all the baptised much greater. This presbyteral role may then of course be added to by purely practical considerations in any specific place, but it must always be remembered that these additional activities are not themselves ordination-specific: they simply arise out of the exigencies of a particular parish ministry. Leaving these things aside, then, the role of the ordained person would appear to be fourfold:

a) to preside at the eucharist.

b) to pronounce absolution and blessing in the name of the Trinity.

c) to be the chief pastor in the parish (though not the only one!)

d) to make available to others a theological and spiritual competence acquired as a result of particular training and 'priestly' (to use the usual and familiar term) formation.

Outside of these very specific things, the whole of Christian ministry is common to all and will be shared by all. What a Seeking Church will therefore recognise is that over the next generation or so there needs to be found a new understanding of the relationships involved in ministry which sees clergy and lay people as entirely equal in a creatively symbiotic relationship, and in which ministry is collaborative. It will do away with the outmoded echoes of caste and status, and recognise that function rather than ontology is the primary distinction. To think like this will empower both clergy and lay people, and has the added benefit that it removes the burden from the ordained minister of thinking (wrongly) that he or she is responsible for everything in ministry. His or her specific responsibilities are actually quite small, and the rest is – or, theologically speaking, should be – shared with the whole people of God. Collaborative ministry is theologically, pastorally and practically, the only model of ministry which recognises both the primary calling of baptism and the very particular calling to ordination and relates them one to the other as complementary equals.

Finally, and by way of conclusion to this outlining of a new approach to ministry, there are two immense practical benefits to be noted, one of which largely applies to the ordained and the other of which has a potentially transforming impact on the church lives of lay people.

As far as the clergy are concerned, they would, in a Seeking Church, find themselves in a changed and, I would argue, spiritually and pastorally much healthier situation. They would be set free in practical terms, as we have mentioned, by the knowledge that ministry is the shared responsibility of all and that it is not all 'up to me', and they would be set free theologically and spiritually by being released from the ontologically-generated burden of caste or status, and knowing themselves to be, as it were, one minister among many. This freedom will allow room for vision and imagination and, on occasion, for a genuinely prophetic ministry.

In a Dispensing Church one does admittedly see rare and shining examples of such ministry, but the overwhelming percentage of clergy in every denomination are, frankly, so completely overworked just in order to 'keep the show on the road' that there is little time and even less energy for reflection, let alone a creative vision or a prophetic voice. These things might, indeed, be one of the most distinctive and far-reaching contributions of a Seeking Church. There is no way of predicting in advance what exact form a visionary ministry might take, and it will in any case vary from place to place and from person to person. One can simply suggest that among its diffuse forms might be such things as new partnerships with local communities on projects of mutual concern, exploration of the theological and spiritual potential of art, music and literature, and a creative willingness to explore new modes and dynamics of parish (and even inter-parish) ministry through the formation of a team-based collaborative approach.

This last possibility, of creative new ways of envisioning and doing ministry, brings us to the second enormous practical benefit of a Seeking Church's approach to ministry. With its collaborative and de-ontological attitude, a Seeking Church will actually do what the priest is enjoined to do in the final section of the ordination charge quoted earlier in this chapter, that is: '... joining with them [the people] in a common witness, that the world may come to know God's glory and love'. As the primary calling to ministry is seen as that of baptism, it becomes clear that the gifts of all, and not just some, are available for the work of ministry in all of its forms, and indeed that the style of ministry in any particular place will almost certainly be shaped by the gifts which are available there. A Seeking Church will therefore actively look for, foster and utilise these diverse gifts, and this is in direct contradistinction to so many Dispensing Churches where the rich talents which are present in every community are almost entirely wasted.

The effect of this discernment and employment of gifts upon the church would be – and already is in the relatively few places where it is done – enormous. Where a Dispensing Church tends to 'de-skill' its members, a Seeking Church will empower them, and many more people will start to feel valued and valuable within the life of the church. Further than this, though, a Seeking Church will, through this process, come to be 'owned' by its members. It is a church in which every individual will have a distinctive contribution, and not, as is all too frequently and sadly the case, a church in which ministry is something which is done to, rather than done by the congregation. But who is this congregation? We have sub-titled this book *A Space for All*, and we must therefore turn in the next chapters to consider not merely a new ministry, but a new scope for the church. It is perhaps here that the church faces its greatest challenge.

CHAPTER NINE

A Space for All – Doctrine

The writing of this book has resembled the climbing of a spiral staircase: topics which we have visited from a primarily theological angle now need re-visiting from the equally important – and infinitely more difficult – practical dimension. Of these the most significant are the openness and inclusivity of a Seeking Church which will occupy us in this and the succeeding chapters, first in terms of the potential membership of a Seeking Church, and secondly in terms of the openness of such a church to other Christian traditions and even other faiths.

Theologically, then, we have argued for an open-ended and inclusive church, but what might this mean in practical terms? I propose to consider this first in principle, and then in terms of a number of concentric circles of difficulty, each of which presents a greater challenge (and/or opportunity?) to the church.

In principle we have argued already that the church should model itself on the openness of Jesus; open, that is, to the outcast, the unloved, the curious, the unlikely. And this openness should be one not merely of toleration, but of compassion, reaching out and, in the end, of love. This does not make for wishy-washyness or an 'anything goes', no standards attitude, as we shall see, and although it may need to be qualified by other factors, this must, I believe, if it is to be true to the nature of its founder and Lord, be the church's initial response to all who would approach.

We can see (and need properly to rediscover) this quality of welcome and love so evident in the Jesus of the gospels. Jesus has compassion on the crowds, he heals their sick, he weeps at the death of Lazarus, and he actively associates with the most

111

unprepossessing (and not infrequently taboo) characters. It seems that the only criterion which qualifies one to be in the presence of Jesus is a wish to be there: nationality, religion, social standing, stigma, lose all of their force in his presence. Desire is all.

So how might this cash out in the life of the church? As mentioned above, I will consider this in the following three chapters, looking successively at areas which pose increasingly awkward problems: these are doctrine, ethics and risk.

First, then, doctrine. Traditionally, as we have seen, doctrine for any church of the broadly Dispensing variety, is the touchstone for membership. Acceptance of the church's doctrinal package allows safe passage into the fold; but denial – or even radical questioning – of any part of it brings criticism, a probable accusation of heresy and, among many denominations, the possibility of expulsion or excommunication.

A corollary of this is that a Dispensing Church is perceived by those on its fringes or outside it looking in as being unwelcoming to those who cannot 'sign up' *in toto*. It is, effectively, a closed club unless the rigid criteria for membership are fulfilled.

This may sound harsh, but pastoral experience convinces me that it is true. For over the years I have found, in each of the parishes in which I have served, 'refugees' from other congregations (even from ones within the same denomination), who have felt squeezed out of their original church because of some disparity of belief or practice between them and the rule-making majority and hierarchy. Indeed, however hard an individual may try to make such people welcome, the sheer weight of the church's perceived rigidity will make it sometimes impossible to succeed. Thus only recently, a young couple who are both definitely on a spiritual journey and feel themselves to be seeking for God, informed me that ultimately they did not feel able to marry in church – not because it was not a meaningful act for them, but because they could not subscribe to every jot and tittle of orthodox Christian belief. And so the rickety old bus (to hark back to the theological students' model) deposited another two pilgrims by the roadside and continued on its worn out, arthritic way!

This archaic and destructive perception of the church needs to change, and change radically, both from within and as it is viewed from outside. Such a change would be ushered in the moment we began, both individually and corporately, to think of ourselves as a Seeking Church rather than a Dispensing Church, for such a church would look and feel very different from the inside, and this in turn would lead to the flowering of a new and more positive conception of it on the part of those on its fringes and even outside it.

At this point I have to concede that such a change looks to be some considerable way off, and it would depend upon a sea-change in our attitude to faith and particularly to the central concept of *agnosis* such as has been both outlined and advocated in the first two volumes of this trilogy.

That said, if such a change were to happen, the effects would be far-reaching indeed, and it is now important, therefore, to consider in some detail how it might feel to be a member of such a Seeking Church, and what its mindset and self-understanding would be.

The first characteristic of such a church would be an overt acknowledgement that it does not have all the answers: that the Christian faith is not a completely closed doctrinal system which leaves no room for manoeuvre or variation of opinion. (Of course, in reality the church never has had all the answers, but the Dispensing Church has tended to make a domineering pretence of claiming to do so.) What this means in practice is that there would be an openly acknowledged greater diversity and interpretation of belief than the church has previously been willing to condone. Thus, for example, to pick up on ideas explored earlier in Chapter Three, there would be the freedom to interpret the Virgin Birth as either fact or myth, acknowledging that there is no definitive scriptural warrant for one standpoint over the other. After all, the 'purpose' of this doctrine is not primarily to require us to believe in a piece of history in the same way that

we 'believe' that the Battle of Clontarf took place in 1014, but to
offer us a window on to the conjoint human and divine nature of
Jesus Christ, and this purpose is served equally well whether we
regard the doctrine as one of historical fact or as one of inspired
myth.

A Seeking Church therefore has, as a primary characteristic,
a more open and tolerant mindset than a Dispensing Church.
The two thousand year history of the Dispensing Church is
littered with anathemas and excommunications and schisms
centred around almost every conceivable point of doctrine, but a
Seeking Church knows that these doctrines are not written for
ever on tablets of stone, but are provisional and are there not as
ends in themselves but as pointers – possibly the best we have so
far – to one aspect or another of the nature or activity of God or
of our relationship with God. Our seeking acknowledges and
values these doctrines but is not imprisoned by them, for there
may always be something more of the 'fullness of truth' to be revealed to us, and a Seeking Church will therefore welcome and
respect all of the varied insights, questions and attempts at elucidation and illumination on the part of its members.

This sense of open-endedness and of ongoing engagement
with the church's doctrines leads naturally to the second characteristic of a Seeking Church, which is that it understands itself,
both individually and corporately, to be a people *in via*, a pilgrim people, just as we have explored towards the end of
Chapter Four. This self-image of a pilgrim people is vital, since it
banishes for ever the ossifying spectre of the church being somehow a 'fixed point'. It is not. It is a people in movement, in flux,
forever journeying onward together, and this allows it to be receptive to people at every stage of their own personal pilgrimage. The club is, as it were, open to new members rather than
being a closed shop.

Being such a pilgrim people brings with it in particular two
positive consequences. First, it allows everyone – no matter
where they are on their journey – to feel that they are equally
valid and valued members of this travelling community.

Inevitably there will be tremendous varieties of faith and commitment. There will be those who have what we might call a 'strong' faith, but equally there will be those with a profoundly questioning, wavering, or even at points doubtful faith. And perhaps above all there will be those who might be termed 'enquirers' – people who are looking in and testing the water to see whether their own spiritual quest might find some sort of a home in this community. Not necessarily always, but certainly far too often, a Dispensing Church will convey an attitude of disapproval – or at least mistrust – towards those who are not firmly committed, and they may find themselves insufficiently welcomed and 'at home', and so drift away again into their own spiritual wilderness. By contrast, a Seeking Church will acknowledge that even within a community gathered around God in Christ there will be many different stages of pilgrimage within that community, and all will be welcomed – as Jesus welcomed all – whatever their needs, doubts, questions or hesitations.

Secondly, a Seeking Church will be able to accept, as a matter of simple spiritual and psychological truth, and not as something negative, that no individual ever stays still on their spiritual journey, and that just as there may sometimes be progress, there may at other times be frustration, dryness or agonising doubt. I presume that my own spiritual experience in life is by no means unique and, if honest, I should have to admit that there has been at least as much of dryness and of doubt as there has been of fulfilment or a sense of the nearness of God's presence. A Seeking Church can encompass these oscillations as being natural and inevitable, without casting upon the individual concerned any taint of 'backsliding' or 'letting the side own'. Indeed, a community which openly acknowledges that our faith may be permanently in flux in this way is thereby more likely to be in a position positively to respond and assist in periods of doubt, dryness or crisis. For in such a community these things need no longer be hidden, but may be freely discussed, and the wisdom and experience of other members of the community sought without fear of disapproval or being made to feel somehow 'second-class'.

Every pilgrim needs, at times, the assistance of the others: this is patently obvious on any demanding physical pilgrimage, and a Seeking Church readily and positively acknowledges that it is so in our equally demanding spiritual pilgrimage.

The third characteristic of a Seeking Church's self-understanding is that it is not only a people *in via*, but that, as a corollary of this, the church itself as a visible institution is, like its statements of belief, entirely provisional. There is nothing, whether ontologically, temporally or physically, immutable about it. To a Dispensing Church this may very well seem tantamount to heresy, and yet it is entirely consonant with the *agnosis* of scripture and with the need (so often overlooked or, for the sake of human comfort, neglected) not to set human limits to the expected – and therefore as we have argued elsewhere, in the case of a kenotic or self-limiting God, the possible – activity of God. The future is God's, and for a Seeking Church, God's it must firmly remain.

Mention has been made here of the *agnosis* of scripture, and although the second volume of this trilogy dealt substantially with this topic, it is worth establishing here just how deeply-rooted and thoroughgoing this *agnosis* is when it comes to such matters as our human future, and therefore, by implication and extension, that of the church also. Two passages from the New Testament are particularly pertinent here.

The first of these comes from the very familiar chapter on love in 1 Corinthians 13. St Paul is extolling the value of love as an abiding way, and he contrasts it with both prophecies and knowledge which will 'pass away'. All, except for love, will be changed in the future, and the reason for this is that everything except love is provisional and subject to divine completion: 'For now we see in a mirror dimly, but then face to face. Now I know in part; then I shall understand fully, even as I have been fully understood.'

Secondly, the author of 1 John comments: 'Beloved, we are God's children now; it does not yet appear what we shall be, but we know that when he appears we shall be like him, for we shall see him as he is.' Here again there is a complete provisionality of knowledge, though not, importantly, of relationship. We are God's children, although we do not know for certain exactly what that will mean for all eternity, and if prophecy, knowledge and our own exact nature and destiny in eternity are all mutable, then how much more so must be the church which is, in itself, only the medium through which we come to apprehend and participate in these things.

It is provisional both in terms of its beliefs and in terms of its structures. The provisionality of its beliefs has been explored in some detail already and needs no further attention here, but what of the provisionality of its structures? This is something to which my own denomination of Anglicanism has at least paid lip service, but even here I do not think that the depth of that provisionality has ever really been fully plumbed and appreciated.

There are, then, at least four ways in which a Seeking Church regards its own structures and indeed identity as being provisional. Of these perhaps the two most radical ones are that any denomination is provisional, and so is the 'visible' nature of the church with its plethora of large and often ancient buildings. A Seeking Church will realise that any given denomination may be required to pass away or be subsumed in the service of a greater unity, as was prophetically done by the formation of the churches of North and South India and the creation of the United Reformed Church in England. Likewise it may be that the church may be required to surrender some or all of its bricks and mortar if, for example, it is ever realised that the burden of maintaining national monuments is draining energy, talent and finance away from things which are more properly constitutive of the church's nature and mission. At any rate, a Seeking Church will 'sit lighter' to this visible presence, realising that – contrary to the message which so often seems to emanate from endless church discussions on the maintenance of property – the church is primarily composed of people rather than real estate.

The other two aspects of the provisionality of its structures are less dramatic but equally far-reaching, and these are simply

an openness towards new patterns of ministry and of church
government, and a recognition of the reviseability of the
church's 'official' pronouncements on any issue – and such a
recognition would, for example, on the part of the Roman
Catholic Church, require a complete abrogation of the doctrine
of papal infallibility.

It should perhaps be stressed here that I am not saying that
any of these four structural elements of the church necessarily
must or will change: it may be that the current denominations
carry on with their present buildings indefinitely. Rather, I am
arguing that for a Seeking Church a permanent openness to the
possibility of change must be there, for where we are now is not
necessarily where God wants us to be tomorrow, and we may
not pre-judge the issue by hailing the *status quo* as being some
kind of divinely sanctioned end-point for the church.

A church which does not have all the answers; a church and
people *in via*; and a church which knows itself to be entirely provisional: if these are three of the primary characteristics of a
Seeking Church then what, it may reasonably be asked, is the
more tangible 'glue' which holds it together? We have substantially answered this question in Chapter Five, but it is useful
briefly to revisit those arguments here in order to draw together
some more threads of the mindset and self-understanding of a
Seeking Church.

Essentially, then, as well as the three characteristics alluded
to already, a Seeking Church knows itself to be identified by and
centred around two foundational elements. First, there is its
commitment not to an exact uniformity of doctrinal interpretation, but to its central shared story: that is, the story of God's
dealings with his people and their response to him as recorded
in scripture, and as pre-eminently revealed in the life, death and
resurrection of Jesus Christ. This story is re-presented in the eucharist, in which is found the heart of the church's identity: its
corporate thanksgiving for, and participation in the story of
Jesus Christ with which all of its contemporary stories in the
lives of its members interweave, and which issues in a call to

service in the world, strengthened by the indwelling presence of Christ through the Holy Spirit.

Secondly, and indeed springing largely from this centredness around a shared story, there is the Seeking Church's sense of being a people bound together by a powerfully relational faith, and finding both their common and individual identities not in dogma but in relationship with God and with each other. Rachel Feldhay Brenner expresses very clearly the importance of relationship and community for the true development of the individual: 'Identity is a function of social interaction. Outside society, identity has no meaning.'[1] In recognising this, the Seeking Church is being not only a church for the future, but also a church which remains true to one of the oldest insights of the Christian church. As Martin Lloyd Williams expresses it so appositely:

> It is the insight of the contemplative tradition, stretching right back to the Desert Fathers, that none of us can find our true selves in isolation from others or from God. In fact there is no such thing as the self apart from relationship with the other.[2]

Thus far we have concentrated exclusively on the internal self-understanding of a Seeking Church – that is, what it looks like to itself. Equally, however, a part of any ecclesiology is the question of how any particular church relates to the world around it, and therefore how it might be perceived by that world. Just as with purely internal matters, here too the Seeking Church has, potentially, a very different – and I would argue more positive – image and impact than the church has often had.

To begin with, its overt acceptance of its own provisionality and its emphasis on a shared story and a relational faith, rather than an unyielding package of dogma, would make the church look a little less like a fortress and rather more like a place of welcome. There would no longer be a sense that if you cannot 'sign up' then you should keep away, but rather that here is a place and community of shared exploration which others are free to enter.

This altered perception would then in turn, I suggest, engender two significant consequences. The first of these would be that the church would then be in a position to reach out to the substantial percentage of people in contemporary society who claim to be 'religious' or 'spiritual' people, but who have no affinity with the church as it at present exists, feeling it to be too much of a 'closed shop'. As I have argued elsewhere, the existence of this very large group of people is well attested to by the burgeoning market in religious publishing even in an age when regular churchgoing is, in general declining. (That this market is expanding is borne out by the fact that at several of the major book fairs in 2007 religious publishing was the largest single category of publishing represented!) Thus there is a definite spiritual hunger 'out there', but the Dispensing Church is not adequately equipped to tap into it or begin to find ways of feeding it.

By contrast, a Seeking Church will be a community within which many such people may find that there is room for their own personal spiritual search. Being a community *in via* it will not demand that people should have reached any fixed point before they are free to come in and 'look around'. Seekers of all shades of theological opinion will be given a genuine welcome. And a Seeking Church will readily acknowledge and accept the fact that some of these seekers will remain whilst others, after a time, will move on. For there will be no coercion to conform, and yet equally there will be no creeping syncretism since, for all its openness, the Seeking Church knows itself to be centred around the eucharist, and therefore indelibly Christo-centric. The seeker whose quest finds a home – however tentatively or questioningly – in Christ may well stay, whilst others, for whom Christ is not yet central, may leave, perhaps nonetheless taking something of faith, or at least of love, with them.

The second consequence would arise as a direct result of this increased movement into and out of the ambit of the church. That is, the church would no longer be perceived as being separate from the rest of society, but as genuinely existing in the midst of it. Thus the church might find itself once again – as the

Dispensing Church was in, say, the medieval period, although in very different circumstances and in a radically different vein – meaningfully connected to the broader fabric of society and therefore better able to witness to it, rather than being regarded, as so often at present, as being in a separate and irrelevant compartment of life.

At the outset of this chapter I mentioned three areas in which the Seeking Church will attempt to provide a 'space for all'. In this chapter we have explored the nature of the doctrinal space in a Seeking Church, and we must now in the succeeding two chapters explore first the ethical space which a Seeking Church allows, and secondly the radical risk which must be embraced by a church which genuinely attempts to create a 'space for all'.

CHAPTER TEN

A Space for All – Ethics

If a Seeking Church needs to find a new openness in matters of doctrine, then in turn it needs to do so – and possibly with even greater urgency – in the realm of ethics. Doctrinal openness may, as we have argued, be far-reaching in its implications, but it is less tangible than any given ethical standpoint which necessarily 'cashes out' in the practical everyday lives of believers, and which identifies the praxis of the church to the world around it.

In ethics, as in doctrine, the Dispensing Church has tended to present a package ready-made for the acceptance (and obedience) of the faithful. And again, as doctrinally, the effects of this have been stultifying and frequently infantilising, as thought and questioning are, to all intents and purposes, outlawed. In the dim and distant past, in an age of widespread illiteracy and ignorance, such an approach might once have been appropriate, but for the past one hundred years at least it has been not only inappropriate but destructive, both for the lives of individual believers and for the corporate life of the church itself. As Victor Griffin, often one of the more prophetic voices in the Church of Ireland, appositely expresses it:

> The greatest change, especially during the latter half of the twentieth century, has been the reluctance to accept pronouncements by ecclesiastical authorities on faith and morals as having divine sanction and therefore to be accepted and obeyed without question. A better informed and articulate laity is now only too ready to question and reject aspects of church teaching, especially on such matters as sexuality, celibacy, ordination etc when they find certain elements lacking credibility in the light of modern knowledge and experi-

ence. If further alienation of membership from the institutional churches is to be avoided, the voice of the questioning
individual, lay person or cleric, needs to be taken seriously
and not promptly dismissed as unworthy of discussion.[1]

In the face of such a critique – which I would roundly echo –
what does the response of a Seeking Church need to be? In
essence, I suggest, it is two-fold: an entirely new method of approaching ethics (which will carry with it certain consequences),
and what I would call a new ethical perception of the church's
own life and mission.

First, then, a new ethical method. In what follows there will
inevitable be a substantial degree of overlap with ideas which I
first expressed in *The Right True End of Love*, but at the risk of repetition it is necessary to re-state at least some of these ideas here
in the present context of the church's self-understanding.

Traditional Christian ethics – at least as it has worked itself
out in the Dispensing Church – has been based, apparently logically, on the foundational ideas of 'right' and 'wrong', and our
ideas about what constitutes right and wrong have largely been
derived from a somewhat naïve reading of scripture and given a
'God says' status of infallibility. There are, however, many problems with this approach, all of which were accorded substantial
treatment in Chapter Five of *The Right True End of Love*. Of these
problems it is sufficient to adduce only two here. Thus the ap-
peal to scripture or to a 'God says' basis for ethics is entirely cir-
cular and has no reference point outside itself to indicate why
God or scripture consider any particular activity to be morally
permissible or not. Likewise the propensity of a Dispensing
Church to deal in morally absolute statements – that such and
such is right or wrong – entirely obscures, or perhaps wilfully
ignores, the fact that the church has changed its mind on ethical
matters, such as what constitutes a valid marriage and, in the
Anglican Church specifically, both divorce and artificial contraception. Viewed in this light, Christian ethics is neither adequately grounded nor unconditionally binding. On the contrary,
it is both open to, and in need of, re-making.

The question therefore is, if it is not, as supposed, with the concepts of right and wrong, where should a specifically Christian ethics start? What may properly be said to be its foundations? The answer which I returned in *The Right True end of Love*, and to which I still adhere, is: in the nature of God himself. Two of the principal qualities which the Christian tradition has consistently ascribed to God, and which appear to be fundamental to God's nature, are creativity and love, and it is in these qualities I argued there, that we are to find the foundations of our ethics. As I expressed it on that occasion, and I have seen no need to amend my position since:

> I am proposing that serious consideration be given by the church to the development of a new model of Christian ethics which is based on the principles of divine (and therefore also of human) creativity and love; and I am proposing also that these principles are (or should be) the touchstones which will provide the logic according to which we will form conclusions as to the acceptability or otherwise of particular actions.[2]

For a Dispensing Church such a style of ethics will almost certainly be unacceptable, because an *a priori* knowledge of 'right' and 'wrong' is part of the given package from which the church dispenses. All we have to do is follow the rules, and it is at least quasi-heretical to suggest that we might need to find out what those rules are first. Within the mindset of a Seeking Church, however, such a starting point for ethics will look much more attractive, since it is not constituted by a set of irrevocable givens, but is always open to revision and re-interpretation and can take in its stride new and hitherto unforeseen ethical issues and dilemmas. Similarly the values and mores of the past may be seen to be entirely, partially, or indeed not at all appropriate in the present and in the future as a people *in via* apply these touchstones of creativity and love to the ethical issues which confront them.

How this approach to ethics actually operates and how it

might influence the church will be explored presently, but first there is one major potential (and misplaced) objection which might be levelled at it by a Dispensing Church, and this must be addressed before we can proceed any further. Thus, because it does not proceed from a given and unassailable set of moral 'oughts' and rules, but rather seeks to work towards a final 'ought' and notions of right and wrong from an understanding of the divine nature, a Dispensing Church will level the charge that an ethics such as this is wishy-washy and 'anything goes': if there are no fixed rules from the outset, then we can decide more or less what we like.

Not so, I would argue. Again as I expressed it in *The Right True End of Love*:

> ... although it does not start from them, it is important to make it very clear that an ethics based on love and creativity does not do away with the concepts of 'right' and 'wrong': that is, it does not lead to a vague and woolly 'anything goes' kind of mentality. On the contrary, the effect of choosing a different starting point is actually to refine (and perhaps even to some extent to re-define) our ideas of right and wrong by providing a much less arbitrary (and much more doctrinally centred) basis for why we decide that certain things are right or wrong. For example, murder and adultery do not suddenly become morally acceptable as a result of a slide into some sort of anarchic moral relativism, but in an ethics of creativity and love they are considered to be wrong not because of any divine *fiat* but because they are destructive of life, love or relationships. It cannot be stressed often enough that this approach to ethics is not a soft option or a cop-out.[3]

If, then, moral judgements can still be meaningfully made, and if they are made not by applying pre-set rules but by interrogating our ethical issues through the medium of divine creativity and love, what implications and effects will this approach have upon a Seeking Church, and how might it change both its self-understanding, its membership and its mission?

Perhaps the most obvious and immediate area in which it
would have an impact is in the church's response to what are
often called 'lifestyle choices', particularly in the realm of
human sexuality, and it is, I believe, no accident that it is precisely
here that, at the present time, a hugely dominant Dispensing
Church is attempting to stifle (and sometimes even to demonise)
a small but growing and, I venture to suggest, prophetic Seeking
Church. Again I have rehearsed the moral arguments for the
validity of homosexuality within a Christian context in *The Right
True End of Love* and there is no merit in repeating them here.
The point on this occasion is that if accepted – as by a Seeking
Church they would be – then the full acceptance of people of a
homosexual orientation into the life, fellowship and ministry of
the church would have significant consequences both for the
membership of the church and for the richness of its communal
insight and wisdom.

That this is so is expressed poignantly and passionately by
David L. Norgard in his essay, 'Lesbian and Gay Christians and
the Gay-friendly Church', and it is especially interesting that in
the second paragraph of this passage Norgard makes it very
clear also that only something like a Seeking Church is ever
going to be one which fully accepts and values gay and lesbian
members in a way that a Dispensing Church, by its very nature,
simply cannot manage to do. He writes:

> The educational program of a healthy church is also appreci-
> ated by gay and lesbian members. No less than straight
> learners, gay and lesbian Christians seek knowledge of holy
> scriptures and sacred traditions, church history and
> Episcopal liturgy. And again, not only do they want to learn,
> they also want to teach. They want to share insights that de-
> rive from their unique relationship with the church and with
> God. They enjoy contributing to the dialogue out of which
> comes new insight and inspiration for all.
>
> Making all this a reality necessitates a significant change
> of mindset, since those already in the church tend to assume
> that they have knowledge, whereas outsiders and newcom-

ers do not. With this mindset, the church becomes the magnanimous purveyor of privileged information. Fully incor-
porating lesbian women and gay men into congregational
life, then, involves a revision of the collective understanding
of church, seeing it not only as a source of knowledge but
also as a body of seekers pursuing truth together.[4]

Even at this stage it begins to appear that only a Seeking
Church will ever be able genuinely to offer a 'space for all'.

But topical – and important, given the potential divisiveness
of the current debate within Anglicanism especially – though it
is, homosexuality is by no means the only 'lifestyle choice' issue
to which a new Christian ethics, and with it a Seeking Church,
might be moved to respond to with a less jaundiced vision than
the present largely Dispensing Church does. Two other areas
(and partly related ones as we shall see) are those of common
law relationships and single-parent families.

The connection between the two lies in the Dispensing
Church's fundamental disapproval of these states of life (often
deeply hidden), and which surfaces only when there is a potential sanction in place. The result is an unpalatable and un-
savoury web of formal politeness masking a moral distaste, and
which leads, not infrequently, to enormous hurt on the part of
individuals, and indeed whole families.

To an ethically traditionally-minded Dispensing Church
both types of lifestyle are ultimately wrong, for both imply (indeed, in the case of single parent families, prove!) the presence
of a sexual relationship outside marriage. All but the most hard-
line must, however, accept the growing prevalence of both
states of life in contemporary society, and therefore their presence in the life of the church. This acceptance may, though, be
partial and grudging, and the true colours of the church are all
too frequently shown when a single parent or common law couple present a child for baptism and find their request refused on
the grounds, however politely expressed, of the immorality of
their own personal lifestyle. And it should be stressed that this is
not overstating things at all: in every parish in which I have ever

served I have ministered to a stream of people who have found themselves rejected on precisely these grounds – and they have come from all of the major denominations, my own included.

By contrast, a Seeking Church, with its rather different understanding of ethics would look very differently upon such people, and would be willing and able to welcome them as fellow pilgrims with their own unique experience, wisdom and spiritual insight – and it would also, potentially and vitally, rehabilitate them as morally responsible, rather than reprehensible, beings. It would do so for different reasons in each case.

With regard to common law relationships, a Seeking Church, freed from a mind-set which simply claims that certain things are irrevocably right and others wrong, would remember that, quite simply, the church has already changed its mind (negatively) on this issue in the past, and therefore there is no intrinsic reason why it should be unable to do so once again and more positively in the present.

Thus until relatively recent times – at least as far as the mid eighteenth century, and only finally definitively altered by the Victorian Marriage Acts of 1844 – the church in both England and Ireland recognised common law marriages as both valid and binding. There was no absolute requirement for a church marriage ceremony as such. Since then, though, the church has largely forgotten this, and has started to frown upon relationships with which it was once perfectly content. It appears that for a Dispensing Church what is, is: but for a Seeking Church what has changed once can be changed again, and it will readily acknowledge the creativity and love which flourish in many such partnerships and, as a result, welcome both them and their offspring to the fellowship of the table as well as to the oft-denied rite of baptism.

In the case of single parents the process of ethical revision is perhaps even more radical, but likewise entirely consonant with an ethics based on perceived divine attributes rather than on supposedly divinely sanctioned rules. It is more radical than in the case of common law marriages because there is no suggestion of any marriage – whether common law or ecclesiastical – being involved. The touchstone here must simply be the qualities of creativity and love to which we have adverted earlier. And the equation is complex. For I am not suggesting that a Seeking Church will automatically endorse every case of single parenthood, for there may be much that is destructive in a relentless policy of 'one night stands' or the continual breaking up of short term relationships for example. But neither will it remorselessly condemn on the simple grounds of singleness. There must be discernment, but there is at least room for the discernment of these qualities of creativity and love both in the relationship between parent and child and in the relationship (whatever form it may take) between parent and partner. There may or may not be moral wrongs involved, but the mere fact of single parentage will no longer constitute in itself a ground for negative judgement and potential exclusion or sanction.

These examples of a new ethical approach to people's lifestyle choices are important, and they will, if implemented, plainly have an impact upon the church's outlook and future membership, but they are not the only areas in which a Seeking Church, with its revised attitude to ethics, will respond very differently to society – and, in turn, look very different to that society – from the ways in which the Dispensing Church has traditionally done.

Thus these lifestyle choice issues are very specific ones, but lying behind them there is a much broader and more far-reaching revisioning and revaluation of society. There is, indeed, a renewed (and in some church circles even a new) engagement with that society. By no means all, but certainly many church congregations exist almost as a sort of club for the like-minded, and I have indeed heard it said as a mark of approbation that the church is made up of 'people like us'. That is, with relatively rare exceptions, the church tends to be 'middle class', and if not purely intellectual, at least having an atmosphere of culture, of a certain amount of learning, and assuming in turn that this is the desirable norm. In an almost entirely unspoken way the church values the comfortableness and unthreateningness of this.

That this is so, and because many congregations have a substantial number of very able people among their number, again
tends to lead to an atmosphere in which people are valued because of what they *are*, because of what their talents – or perhaps
even their mere presence – can bring to a church community.
Admittedly this is not inevitable in a Dispensing Church, but it
is a fairly common pattern.

The question arises, then, why does this often come to be the
case in a Dispensing Church, and what is there about a Seeking
Church which would engender a different and more all-embracing attitude? In what follows it should be stressed that I am not
claiming that every Dispensing Church congregation is as I describe, or that a Seeking Church will effortlessly and unfalteringly
change everything instantly for the better. I am merely exploring what, at varying levels of intensity, is too frequently the case
with the largely Dispensing Church of today, and what aspir-
ations we might have if the Seeking Church of tomorrow were to
come more convincingly to birth.

The problems which beset a Dispensing Church in its engagement with society – and with some of its own members – then,
would appear to be threefold. First, there is the matter of doctrine
which, I have consistently argued, should be a second order entity,
but which the Dispensing Church keeps firmly at the centre of
things – after all, it is one of the key things which that church is
able to dispense! Doctrine, though, is inevitably related to one's
ability to digest and understand it, and the Dispensing Church
therefore unintentionally, but still in a way which is discrimin-
atory, places a premium on intellectual ability. The heavily doctrinal focus of the church favours the intellectually able and those
who are at home with the articulation of concepts and ideas.
They are the ones who can most readily learn the 'secrets of the
trade' and who therefore come to be valued above others who
perhaps cannot do so. It is a little like a computer or Playstation
game with its 'levels' – the further you get the better you show
yourself to be. There is, like it or not, an intellectual elitism which
is alive and well in many parts of the church.

Secondly, and as we have seen both in this volume and in *A Space for Unknowing*, related to this rigid doctrinal *schema*, there is the equally rigid moral universe of the Dispensing Church. Quite simply, the presence of a very strong set of pre-existent ethical rules and the consequent habit of labelling things, with little further reflection, as being right or wrong, will often lead to a judgemental mind-set which expresses itself in quasi-ethical judgements even when the issue at stake is not primarily an ethical one. Lest this sound a somewhat far-fetched or exaggerated claim, I should add that it may be readily illustrated from my own experience, and the incident which follows is only one of many which might be adduced.

I served my curacy in the parish of Redcar in the industrial north-east of England at a time when employment in traditional heavy industry was plummeting. Almost as I arrived there, British Steel reduced its workforce by approximately 65%, and there were also huge redundancies at the neighbouring ICI Wilton chemical plant. Not only were thousands rendered unemployed, but school leavers were emerging into a society where there were, literally, no jobs available. Returning to my native Surrey for a New Year break, I well remember an uncle of mine holding forth on the subject and accusing these same school leavers of laziness, lack of ambition and so forth and, effectively, branding them as worthless layabouts. Knowing many of the people as I did, I confess that I have rarely been so angry! A moral judgement had been passed on fully 30% of my parishioners, and on an entirely non-moral issue.

The corollary of this tendency to look down in judgement on certain sections of the population (and also related to putting a premium on intellectual ability) forms the third problem which the Dispensing Church has in its engagement with, and mission to, society. This is its predisposition not only to judge but to patronise, and thereby to alienate.

This arises directly from its sense of being the 'magnanimous purveyor of privileged information' as David L. Norgard felicitously expressed it above. That is, almost without knowing it, the

Dispensing Church, because it knows itself to be the repository of the requisite package of faith and ethics, becomes progressively more patronising as it moves down the intellectual or social scale. Increasingly people simply need to be told exactly what to believe and how to behave. There is no possibility of input, no possibility of dialogue: there is only obedience – or, of course, rejection.

All of these things mean that a Dispensing Church is compromised and hampered in its ministry both to those outside it, and indeed, to a substantial percentage of those inside it. Over against this, however, is the potential for new outreach and a more deeply inclusive pastoral ministry offered by a genuinely Seeking Church. Again there are perhaps three key aspects of such a church which need to be considered.

First, there is the matter of the centrality of story rather than doctrine within the life of the Seeking Church. Just as doctrine has the potential to exclude, so story has the potential for an almost limitless inclusion. Not everyone may be able to appreciate the finer points of doctrine, but everyone – quite literally everyone – has a story, and there is therefore the potential for that story to interact with the story of Jesus Christ, with the stories of other believers, and with the story of the church's communal life. And, both interestingly and significantly, the story of Jesus in particular will tend to be powerfully inclusive of the stories of those who might otherwise find themselves marginalised: the troubled, the handicapped, the less socially advantaged and so on. For the Seeking Church their stories are valid – as valid as those of anyone else, and they have as much right to weave in and out of the story of Jesus and the fellowship of his table. In a Seeking Church there is truly, 'neither Jew nor Greek, there is neither slave nor free, there is neither male nor female; for you are all one in Christ Jesus' (Galatians 3:28).

Secondly, and clearly linked to this mutual interweaving of stories, there is the fact that the other primary locus of a Seeking Church is the relational nature (rather than the primarily dogmatic nature) of its understanding of faith. Again (and perhaps with very rare and inexpressibly sad exceptions) everyone can relate, both horizontally and vertically. Horizontally this is patently obvious when one looks at families with physically or mentally disadvantaged members, or at organisations such as Rotary International which, by its categories of membership, deliberately crosses any pre-conceived social boundaries. Likewise in terms of a relationship with God it is equally true, and the most apparently surprising people can turn out to have a powerful and profound spirituality, whether the socially 'inferior' such as Brother Lawrence, or the mentally afflicted as is borne out by such things as the experience of Jean Vanier with the L'Arche communities or the work of the Camphill Trust. Indeed, a paradigm for such inclusion – albeit on a purely horizontal level – was recently displayed by a Limerick secondary school which rejoiced *en masse* when a pupil with Down's Syndrome successfully completed her Leaving Certificate examination. From the perspective of the life of the church, words of Jesus come sternly and challengingly to mind: 'Go and do thou likewise!'

Thirdly, and over-archingly, the Seeking Church's ethical foundations of creativity and love (rather than a set of governing rules which are simply applied) has its part to play in the ability of that church to reach out and embrace so many who currently find themselves either unloved or ignored. The reason for this is simple: if these two qualities, rather than rules, are allowed to move to the foreground of ethics, then a Seeking Church will realise that they are, potentially, qualities which may characterise the lives of all people – their manifestation does not depend upon ability, 'normality', success, or anything else of this kind, but rather upon relationships and the ability of one person's story to interact meaningfully with that of another person or community.

Contrary to the problems of engagement experienced by a Dispensing Church, a Seeking Church will foster a community in which, in all of the above ways, there is room for input from and dialogue with people of all mental, physical and social shapes and sizes. The aspiration of such a church is that it will be 'owned' by all and provide a 'space for all'.

But even this intellectual and social broadening of horizons is not enough. This will be seen particularly clearly and possibly provocatively in the succeeding chapter, but even within the present parameters of our argument there is a need to ask questions about not only the social and intellectual make-up and outreach of the church, but also about its overtly moral identity.

Jesus told many stories of Pharisees and sinners, and I cannot help feeling that the Dispensing Church is largely constituted by Pharisees – not, of course, in their hypocrisy, but rather in their conviction (usually probably justified) of righteousness. Thus the church, of whatever denomination, is likely – for all the reasons of rules and so on which we have discussed earlier – to be made up of the at least moderately respectable and virtuous, and there is a prevailing sense that anyone currently outside has to become a PLU (person like us) in order to gain entry. Conversion (both of belief and of life) is seen as a requirement of, rather than a consequence of membership.

A Dispensing Church is necessarily thus orientated, simply because some sort of acceptance of its doctrinal and ethical package is a necessary requisite of membership. By thus demanding a membership-dependent change of life it renders itself far less effective in reaching out to the marginalised or the less respectable. Conversely, a Seeking Church is infinitely better placed to do just this. It can issue an entirely open invitation, based on story and relationality, for people to come and explore how their story, their relationships, may interweave with and be moulded by the stories of their fellow seekers and pre-eminently by the story of Jesus Christ. And the invitation is open: for some, their stories and relationships may be dramatically changed by the encounter (what we might otherwise call conversion); for others the experiment may prove unfruitful or a failure, and they will drift away seeing no connection. But the invitation has been made: you do not have to be perfect (or even anywhere near it) to come inside.

Such an approach seems to me to mirror the all-inclusive ministry and mission of Jesus himself. How many times are we told, for example, that he was criticised for associating with 'tax collectors' and 'sinners'? And who, I wonder, are the tax collectors and sinners of today? Whoever they are, the Seeking Church will need to be (and I believe would willingly be) open enough to practise, and not merely to preach, that the church is a community for sinners – within which, and not necessarily prior to entering which, they find redemption and 'amendment of life'. Again the words of Jesus echo hauntingly down the centuries: 'For I came, not to call the righteous, but sinners' (Matthew 9:13).

In all of these ways, then, the Seeking Church is better equipped for mission and pastoral outreach that a Dispensing Church, and in the course of this chapter we have argued the case for a Seeking Church providing a space for many, but what might a 'space for all' ultimately mean? To this daunting question we must now, however hesitantly, turn.

CHAPTER ELEVEN

A Space for All – Risk

In the context of a Dispensing Church the notion of risk is, on the whole, an unacceptable one. The church, in common with all institutions, is innately conservative and resistant to change, and it does not feel comfortable with ventures whose outcomes are unknown. It is a great deal less stressful to stick with the present settled membership and the round of worship and a still largely clerical ministry than it would be to risk a very different style of ministry and a new outreach to people who are definitely not 'people like us'.

But this is precisely the kind of step which a Seeking Church knows it must take if it is truly to provide a 'space for all'. Furthermore, the idea of being a church which embraces risk is not a decision which is made randomly or in a spirit of recklessness or foolhardiness. There is a coherent rationale for it which should be briefly outlined before we proceed any further.

It is almost a truism to say that the church is called primarily to reflect what it understands to be the nature of God in its communal life and in its ministry, both ordained and lay. This involves the living-out of a wide variety of divine qualities, for example the love and creativity which we have already dwelt on at some length, and also other qualities such as compassion, forgiveness, generosity, humility, willing service and so on. So much is obvious, and to do it justice, the church – of however firmly a Dispensing variety – has always tried to manifest these qualities in the lives of its members and thereby also in its own corporate life.

But what is usually either overlooked or ignored is that God is also profoundly a God of risk. I have explored this aspect of

the nature of God at some length in Chapter 6 and there is no
need to rehearse those same arguments again here, other than to
add that I am by no means alone in calling attention – in the context of pastoral outreach – to this aspect of God's nature. Writing
precisely on this topic of pastoral ministry some years ago,
Christopher Moody expressed it thus:

> ... God himself has taken the risk of identifying his own hon-
> our with the fortunes of his people. God, as it were, risks his
> reputation on his people's obedience to the agreement he has
> made with them, an obedience which is potential rather than
> actual.[1]

This being so, is it not incumbent upon the church to take
risks in the name of this risk-taking God? I suggest that this
must be so, and for two reasons. The first is that to do so is simply to reflect another aspect of the nature of God in exactly the
same way as the church has always tried to live out the divine
attributes of compassion, forgiveness and so on. If it is to be true
to what it perceives as the fullness of God's nature, then this at-
tribute, no less than any other, needs to be reflected in the
corporate life of his people.

Secondly, and equally importantly, it is only through risk
that the church will be able to fulfil its calling of preaching the
gospel to all people. Risk is, for the church, as for God, a necessary pre-condition of possible success. For God the risk is ongoing. That is, it appears to us that God's purpose in creation was
the bringing about of beings able freely to respond to love with
love. But for this to be possible those beings have to be truly free.
And in this lies the risk: the risk of failure; the risk (realised
countless millions of times throughout the history of humanity)
that at any moment any of these beings can reject their creator's
purpose and turn away from him. Similarly, for the church also,
the possibility of success entails risk: the risk of becoming vulnerable and open to rejection, pain or opprobrium, and, of
course, the risk of failure. But, as we shall see, it is only by taking
such risks that the church can aspire to provide a 'space for all'

and fully empower all of its members and engage with society and its many pressing issues.

So, having established the rationale for a risk-taking church, what is the nature of these risks? What is it, more specifically, that the church is being asked to embrace? In general terms the risks involved encompass two broad areas: these being first, the mission and potential membership of the church, and secondly the nature and pattern of its ministry. However, before embarking on an exploratory tour of these two areas it should be pointed out that in what follows it is not possible to be comprehensive or in any way prescriptive. This is simply because the precise nature of the risks which will need to be taken will vary from congregation to congregation, and also because what may appear as new, unknown and potentially risky territory to one congregation may already be part and parcel of the day's business for another congregation.

With this proviso in mind, then, what at least are some of the broad parameters of risk which will need to be accepted by a church which has a vision of a 'space for all'? With regard to the mission and membership of the church, the risks to be taken will clearly vary enormously from place to place, but essentially the risk is one of being permanently challenged to go beyond the church's corporate comfort zone and offer ministry and mission to those with whom any particular congregation does not normally feel comfortable. The three examples offered here are by no means exhaustive, but they do reflect the nature of the task and challenge facing the church.

First, then, one very simple thing which causes us to feel vulnerable, sometimes wary and even mistrustful or fearful, is difference: that is, a radical difference of lifestyle, culture or outlook from those with which we are familiar. Many communities in contemporary Ireland are learning rapidly and of necessity about the presence of difference, and about the difficulties and rewards of assimilating it. The difference in our newly multicultural and multi-racial Ireland may be one of nationality and culture, or of religion, or of lifestyle. As far as nationality is concerned there are substantial populations of Poles, Latvians, Lithuanians, Brazilians, Nigerians, Chinese and many more in different parts of the country. Likewise we are now living along- side increasing numbers of Moslems, Hindus, Sikhs, Buddhists and so on. And in terms of lifestyle difference there is, for exam- ple, still a substantial travelling community whether on the roads or in council provided halting sites.

Reaching out to any of these groups across the boundaries of difference may make a church feel uncomfortable and uneasy, but it needs to be done and the risk of rejection (or of having one's safe, familiar community changed) accepted. And this reaching out will not always be of a directly church-oriented 'mission' variety – indeed this will often be inappropriate alto- gether, as when someone comes from a different denomination or even religion. Genuine reaching out will involve a simple welcome to newcomers, both to a church and to a community, and there are a myriad ways of doing this such as a visit or a welcoming card. Beyond this the church could play a major part in assisting newcomers to feel 'at home' in their new environ- ment: possibilities might include language classes, childcare facilities, an inter-faith study group, or assistance with endless bureaucratic form-filling in a strange language.

Likewise, within the ambit of the church itself there are very concrete ways to reach out and welcome the newcomer, the dif- ferent. Are there, for example, cherished prayers or hymns which have travelled with them and which might be learned and used? Is anyone willing to help them negotiate the pitfalls of an unfamiliar prayer-book? Are they invited to and welcomed at whatever activities the church runs apart from worship? It may be that many congregations are doing some or all of these things already, but for many others there is still the risk of difference to be faced and overcome.

Secondly, as well as this general sense of difference, there may be any number of place-specific risks to be embraced if the church is to reach out genuinely to all. Thus a particular parish may contain a prison, a mental health unit, an addiction counselling centre or whatever. And in these circumstances the risk is more tangible and certainly stronger than that of mere difference. Prisons, and their inmates, for example, may appear threatening, and the task of entering one seem completely daunting, or we may be afraid of people with mental disorders or drug addictions, frightened of what they may say or do. But all of them are people, children of the same God, and somehow the church's remit must be to offer to include them.

The means to do this will almost certainly vary from institution to institution and from place to place. Thus a prison may well welcome a competently trained visiting or 'befriending' team and, having done such work myself in Oxford Prison as an ordinand, I know that such visits are valued by a substantial number of prisoners who may be lonely, frightened, depressed or whatever. By contrast, such direct contact will almost certainly be entirely inappropriate in the case of a counselling centre, but even here the offer of inclusion can be extended by the provision of a notice or a supply of A5 flyers detailing church services or meetings. There may be little or even no 'result' from these overtures of inclusion, but that is not the point. What is vital is that the church, which claims to act in the name of Christ and in the power of his Spirit, is extending his call and the news of his love to all.

If these first two groups show increasing evidence of the church's potential commitment to risk-taking in its outreach and inclusion, then the final group which I have chosen to use as an example carries this risk-taking to what may seem to some to be almost rash lengths – and yet I believe that it is still the only genuinely Christ-like way for the church to proceed.

In his own ministry Jesus frequently approached, and was approached by, those whom others were afraid to be near or to touch, and among such groups most notably by lepers. There was good reason why people feared and shunned them, for their disease was debilitating, ultimately fatal, and contagious. Yet on a variety of occasions Jesus was to be found in their company, touching and healing.

Even today lepers are still with us: that is, our society still contains groups of people who are feared and shunned, and there is a major question as to how the church may best reach out to them. Two groups spring immediately to mind, and may be considered successively: these are first, people who are HIV positive, and secondly convicted sex offenders.

The situation of HIV positive people is perhaps not quite as acute as it was a few years ago when the condition carried a quite appalling social stigma, but I do wonder just how many church communities have actively made moves to educate themselves about the condition and to welcome and support individuals who have, for whatever reason, contracted it.

For there is a real need for such ministry. HIV positive people may need supporting through fear or anger, and for any who develop AIDS there will be a need for pastoral care during increasing illness, hospital visiting and so on.

Yet more difficult, though, is the business of offering pastoral care and outreach to convicted sex offenders – difficult and dangerous because it does carry a risk of harm to the church community, and this may rule it out of court for some people. I confess that I have a good deal of sympathy with this attitude, for I can well understand the wariness which undergirds it. Very clear safeguards and precautions may well need to be set in place by a church community, but if we are to be true to the Christ who associated with lepers, then I do not see how our very natural fear can be allowed to have the last (and un-Christlike) word.

On a subject as difficult and delicate as this, some clarification is perhaps needed. Thus I am not suggesting that the church indiscriminately opens its arms and becomes a place of refuge (and possibly plunder) for every potentially dangerous offender. Rather, I am thinking of an imaginary scenario, but nonetheless a potentially very real one – and, who knows, perhaps it has already happened to some congregation somewhere. Thus, what happens if someone who is on the sex offenders register comes to live in our parish, expresses remorse for past

deeds, claims to live an amended life, and seeks to become an active worshipping member of the parish? The church may need
to be extremely careful how it handles (indeed manages) such a
person, but can it truly, in the name of Christ, send them away?
If it does, then the message which goes out with it is that it is
possible to step entirely outside (and irrevocably so) the ambit of
God's love, and surely this is neither theologically nor pastorally
what the church is called to proclaim. For all the risks involved,
the only Christ-like thing to do is to put out one's hand and
allow the leper to shake it as a sign of being rehabilitated into a
community which genuinely does contain a 'space for all'.

In all of these areas connected with mission and membership
it goes without saying that the whole enterprise must be undergirded with the church's regular prayer and worship, both corporate and individual. There will need to be prayer for discernment and wisdom, for grace, and for the ability and willingness
to listen to the stories of others. It is no easy task, but it is the task
of any church which would be Christ's hands and feet and heart
on earth today.

At the outset of this chapter I mentioned that there were two
broad areas in which a Seeking Church will be committed to a
degree of risk taking. Thus far we have explored what this might
mean in terms of mission and membership, and we must now
turn to examine the implications of risk for the nature and pattern of the church's ministry.

Just as with mission and membership, a Dispensing Church
finds ministerial risk-taking very hard to embrace. The church
has its ministry (largely clerical) and its task is to feed the faithful and ensure that the 'right' faith and the 'right' ethics are im-
parted to and imbued by them. Indeed it can sometimes seem as
if 'Thou shalt not rock the boat' was the eleventh commandment
which Moses inexplicably and inadvertently forgot to bring
down from the mountain.

For a Seeking Church risk is part and parcel of ministry, just
as it is of mission. We have considered in a previous chapter
something of the need to declericalise the church – or at least to

empower the ministry of all of its members – and it is now time to revisit this territory and view it through a slightly different lens as it forms the first of two broad areas in which a Seeking Church embraces risks in its ministry.

In traditional models of ministry there is a good deal of 'control'. Ministry – or at least most of it – is in the hands of a relatively few people, and the role of the clergy is at once fairly clearly defined (in terms of providing pastoral care and presiding at the worship and sacraments of the church) and to some degree accountable both to a congregation and to the bishop. Ministry operates largely through known, tried and tested institutionalised channels.

It is therefore innately much more risky to empower the 'ministry of all the baptised' such as we have argued a Seeking Church will do. For immediately ministry becomes far less centralised and more diffuse and it is infinitely harder to 'keep tabs' on it. This is so in a wide variety of ways, and here just three examples will suffice to illustrate at least some of them.

Study groups or house groups of some sort are a familiar feature of church life, but their programme of study is usually 'supervised' in some way by the clergy, and indeed the clergyperson may well be present at (and not infrequently lead) such a group. A fully empowered and confident laity would, however, be more than capable of generating such groups for themselves, and potentially more of them than any clergyperson could ever hope successfully to 'keep an eye' on. Freed from such constraints, such groups might very well come to discuss (and even espouse) ideas which a more conservatively led Dispensing Church would have frowned upon. What is certain is that in such groups (and also privately as individuals) there would be a new freedom to question the church's teaching and to demand some latitude of opinion in matters both of doctrine and of ethics.

Secondly, if lay people are given, corporately, the task of ministry then they will undoubtedly develop their own ideas and have their own personal strengths. This is immensely enriching for the church, but it comes with its own particular price of discomfort. For not all members of a church may be easy with the plethora of directions in which ministry is likely to be exercised as a result of making ministry fully the provenance of all. It may be that there is a personal initiative taken of reaching out to one of the various groups discussed earlier in this chapter, and with whom at least some (if not many) of the congregation feel acutely uncomfortable. New initiatives may lead to stresses and tensions within the church as new ideas or new people enter its ambit and need, over time, to be assimilated.

Thirdly, there may simply be mistakes in ministry in which, however unintentionally, hurt is caused and pastoral harm done. Pastoral care is not always easy, and saying (or not saying!) the right thing can never be guaranteed, and there may be errors of judgement along the way. This is a very real risk, but it should not be over exaggerated. Even a Dispensing Church with its largely clerical ministry is not immune from pastoral error, and it is merely inevitable that the more people are actively involved in ministry the more scope there is for error, just as there is more potential for increased and more widespread care within the community. The risk is simply (as we have argued earlier) the obverse of the rich potential for achievement.

If the setting free of the 'ministry of all the baptised' is the first area of ministerial risk to which a Seeking Church is willing to commit itself, then the second is the overall character of that ministry: that it is prophetic and dynamic.

'Prophetic' is a word which needs closer analysis. It is today a popular (in some circles at least) word to use in connection with ministry, and indeed at conferences on ministry it tends to become something of a 'buzz word'. Too often, though, it is hard enough to assign any precise content to it. So what might it mean in the context of a Seeking Church and its acceptance of risk?

I suggest that it is a term which has implications, just indeed as the Old Testament prophets did, both for those within the community of the faithful and for the world beyond. In large measure these implications – as with the missional risks we have examined – involve risk because a ministry which is prophetic is one which will keep people right on the boundaries of, and not infrequently outside of, their comfort zones. Again we may turn to Christopher Moody for an excellent analysis of this process:

> ... anyone who is put in the position of disclosing God's faith-fulness in leadership is open to the ... dimension of risk. Because the outcome of God's commitment is not yet certain, to come between God and his people as a leader is inevitably to accept the risk of incurring anger, misunderstanding and rejection.
>
> This sense of risk is intrinsic to the biblical imagery. To be a shepherd is to be God's fellow worker in leading his people in the wilderness, keeping watch over them, anticipating their needs, keeping them on the move. The Bible's under-standing of God's relationship with his people under the terms of the covenant is a dynamic one. It is always breaking down, being renewed and opened up to a greater fulfilment. This carries with it the corollary that any pattern of ministry and leadership which encourages people to settle down rather than stay on the move is liable to become obstructive. To use modern jargon, the biblical understanding of pastor-ing is proactive rather than reactive. It is not a matter of keep-ing people where they are, but of keeping pace with God where he is leading.[2]

This in turn involves, by definition, being constantly open to both the challenges and the potential opened up by the new; open to the possibility that something previously unthought of might stem from the prompting of the Holy Spirit. Such open-ness to the new is powerfully and profoundly in line with the biblical conception of prophetic ministry: imagine the initial consternation and distaste when Jeremiah told the people of Israel to pray for their Babylonian captors, or when the minor prophets such as Amos, Hosea and Micah denounced the empti-ness of temple worship.

Thus to take a few contemporary examples (some of which we have touched on previously), I would argue that parts of the church have been genuinely prophetic in ordaining women; that the diocese of New Hampshire has been prophetic (if not necessarily worldly wise or tactful) in electing Gene Robinson as bishop; and that individual congregations and clergy are being prophetic as increasingly they 'break down the barriers which divide' and share at a local level in prayer, in common action, and even (at the risk of displeasing hierarchies) the sacraments.

To add to these examples there will undoubtedly be many more in the future, some of them local and place-specific, others of them affecting much larger sections of the church. In particular I would suggest that the ecumenical and inter-faith sphere (of which more of both in the next chapter) and the relationship between, and roles of lay and ordained ministry leading to a genuinely collaborative approach to ministry are two of the prime areas for a prophetic approach in the future as far as matters internal to the church are concerned.

Finally, then, we must turn to the outward implications of a prophetic ministry: that is, how the church might serve as prophet for society. Here we may discern four major roles for the church, although there may well be further ones which it will require the discernment of others properly to identify.

First, then, there is the church's ability, if the need arises, to speak with a counter-cultural voice. This is something which the Dispensing Church certainly has done from time to time, but which it has emphatically failed to do consistently. There have been long periods in the history of the church when it has been comfortably embedded in society and, sharing its power and prestige, been conveniently blind to even its most reprehensible moral failings. Indeed, it has often gone against the innately conservative grain of that church to act prophetically.

A Seeking Church is not so constrained, for, knowing itself to be a people *in via* it has far less to gain from being identified with the current structures of any particular society. There really is a gap between them, and with modifications, St Augustine's *civitas dei* and *civitas terrena* may genuinely exist side by side. And the vital thing is that the one reserves the right to criticise the other.

Clearly it is not possible to say what the grounds for this criticism may be in any given society. And they may indeed be international, national or merely local. All that can be done here is to indicate some of the ways in which contemporary western – and specifically Irish – society might be open to such a critique. These would include: concern for the poor in a rampantly success-orientated society, this to be complemented by a critique of a wealth and success-based culture; a passionate critique of inflammatory words, attitudes and actions both within the Christian denominations and even more pressingly on the world stage, between Christianity and Islam; and a challenging exposé of the ways in which financial gain prompts ethical quiescence – prime examples being investment in the arms trade and internet child pornography. And this is to say nothing of pressing ecological issues, although admittedly the church as a whole can say little about these until it has removed the beam from its own eye.

If this counter-cultural identity is the first mark of the Seeking Church's prophetic ministry, then the second is its obverse: that some of the values of that church should be proclaimed as potentially valid and biding for society as for the church itself. Essentially we have argued consistently throughout that the church must aspire to provide a 'space for all' and this is an aspiration which the church must in turn press onto society. All societies are very efficient – whether intentionally as in the case of Hitler and the Jews, or merely tacitly as is the case with the poor in many countries – at creating groups of marginalised and 'unimportant' people who can, on the whole, be conveniently shut out and forgotten. Quite simply, for a Seeking Church, itself inclusive of all, this must not be. There can be no 'pale' on any grounds.

The third and forth marks of a Seeking Church in terms of its prophetic witness to the world in a sense flow from this insistence upon a space for all, in that they consist of two complement-

ary proclamations about the 'space for all' created once and for
all by the life, death and resurrection of Jesus Christ, whose own
inclusive ministry is, as we have seen, the ultimate paradigm for
that of the Seeking Church.

The third mark, then, runs parallel to the above concern with
the marginalised, but perhaps bites even more deeply, and this
is to insist on the value, not only of groups, but of each and every
individual. Society, like the church, has no outcasts. This challenge to inclusivity is to be issued overtly in the name of Jesus
Christ, whose death and resurrection were not for some 'in
group' but for all humanity. Admittedly, just as it would appear
that we have the free will to enable us to reject our part in that
death and resurrection, so too it is true that individuals have the
will and the ability to put themselves, effectively, beyond the
reach of society. But that is not the point. The point is that society, like the church and like Jesus Christ himself, must never be
the mechanism of exclusion.

A corollary of this, in that it provides hope for all (even for
those who currently exclude themselves) is the fourth mark of
the prophetic Seeking Church.This is a vision most movingly expressed in Georges Bernanos' classic novel, *The Diary of a
Country Priest*, in which, speaking of the appalling situations of
evil and distress evoked by a Gorki novel, he concludes by saying:

..yet I feel that such distress, distress that has forgotten even
its name, that has ceased to reason or to hope, that lays its tor-
tured head at random, will awaken one day on the shoulder
of Jesus Christ.[3]

and it also provides what is possibly the ultimate *telos* of such
a church, which is to be an agent of God's kingdom and thereby
an agent of transformation. For this fourth mark is nothing less
than the proclamation of the ongoing possibility of transformation, a possibility given to us in the death and resurrection of
Jesus Christ: a possibility of new life, new hope, both here and
hereafter, for the individual, for society, and for the world. A

Seeking Church in via to this goal of transformation both personal and corporate will never allow either itself or the world (insofar as this lies within its power) to be satisfied with any *status quo* of imperfection. If God's kingdom is to be realised even a little more fully, then there is always one more step to be taken into God's unknown and risky future.

In all of these realms, then, and perhaps in many others here unperceived also, the Seeking Church will be a church committed not only to openness (as we have seen in the preceding two chapters) but also to risk-taking in the name of a God of risks, and as the condition of a truly faithful and Christ-like ministry and life. The corollary of this, as we have observed earlier, is that not every experiment will succeed, not every new thing will be from the Holy Spirit, not every decision will be correct, and a Seeking Church will avowedly be a church which makes mistakes. But, in faithfulness to a dynamic God who took the biggest risks of all in creation and Incarnation, it is better to be a church which repents of its errors and journeys forward again than to be a church whose only error is the fatal one of standing still.

CHAPTER TWELVE

Of No Fixed Abode

Thus far we have explored, at least briefly, some of the contours of a Seeking Church. We have analysed the nature of its faith, and attempted to articulate something of its own self-understanding as a pilgrim people, and as an ever-shifting and evolving and so always open and inclusive community. In the course of this we have considered both its ministry and its mission, and identified it as a community united around the person and story of Jesus Christ, and willing, in his name, to take risks in the service of its calling.

In any approach to ecclesiology, however, and this one is no exception, there remains one further issue to be addressed and a set of questions to be answered. These concern the matters first, of how the various churches which together make up the whole body of the church relate to one another, and secondly of how, corporately, Christianity relates to other faiths and in particular to the other major world faiths.

At the present time the lookout on both fronts is decidedly uncertain. Ecumenical gains have been made in recent decades, but to set against this there has been much recent talk of an 'ecumenical winter', and for all the various talks and even joint worship in such places as Assisi, the world faiths (Christianity included) still radiate the overriding impression that each of them is convinced of its own rightness and views the others as, at best (and if indeed relations at all) poor relations.

The picture is sombre as far as any wholly positive outcome is concerned, and indeed it is hard to see just how and why it is likely to change significantly and, for a Dispensing Church, there is an internal logic at work which dictates that it probably will not do so. This logic is integral to the whole mindset of the Dispensing Church. It is never exactly spelt out, and indeed if put as bluntly as it is to be put here, many people might throw up their hands and say, 'But surely my church isn't like that!' But actually, it is: not explicitly perhaps, but implicitly nonetheless. And the mindset is one which says, effectively, that we have the whole deposit of truth (as every good Dispensing Church should have!) and we know what is to be believed and what doctrine and ethics are expected of members. What, then, is there left to learn from others? Indeed, if anything our business should be to teach them and lead them into the fullness of truth which we already possess and are ready to dispense to any who will listen. The only trouble is that every Christian denomination and each of the faiths think in this same way! It is a little like the old joke of the battleship and the lighthouse, and although in theory flexible in their positions, none of the ecclesial or world faith battleships will manoeuvre until it is too late and a collision is inevitable.

The picture remains sombre if only one or merely a few of the Christian denominations adopt a Seeking Church mentality, for the Seeking Church will have to reach a 'critical mass' before it gains enough momentum to influence either the denominational or inter-faith arenas significantly. All that can be hoped and prayed for is that the shift will come, as I believe it will some day.

In all that follows, then, there is the voice of hope rather than of present day reality. We have argued throughout this trilogy that there are signs of change in both theology and church, and it may be that today's hope will become tomorrow's reality.

If it succeeds fully in emerging from its present cocoon, then, how would the presence of a Seeking Church transform both ecumenical and inter-faith dialogue and praxis? From what has gone before, both in this volume and in the preceding ones, the outline of the position to be advocated here should already be clear. In these three volumes, then, we have charted a new (and in some respects also the rediscovery of an old) course for

Christianity amidst the reefs and shallows of doctrine and ethics. We have consistently argued that to remain relevant to the thought patterns and belief structures of believers – and certainly of countless would-be seekers also – the church needs to move away from an overly strict doctrinal approach to faith. Its creeds, its dogmas, and especially its narrowly confessional expressions of belief need to assume a second order status rather than the first order status which they have traditionally held.

As they decrease other things must increase and occupy a place long denied them. Currents which have flowed hidden beneath the surface must come to the surface at last. Specifically, *agnosis*, provisionality and a genuine sense of the church as a people *in via* must displace any sense of the church as settled, definitively knowing and immutable. If these things change then its whole self-understanding will change also, and the church will learn to see itself as a community whose faith is primarily relational and which is gathered around a shared story which has the story of Jesus Christ, the gathering around his table, and the presence of the Holy Spirit as its focus.

The ramifications of this for ecumenism would be, to put it mildly, cataclysmic – but only if, as mentioned earlier, a 'critical mass' of churches were to subscribe to some such perspective. In essence, a Seeking Church would bring about two major changes in ecumenical perspective, both stemming from the open, provisional, agnostic and relational nature of that church. The first of these would be that no denomination would need to feel defensive about its own position or aggressive towards the different positions of others. This would be so because no denomination would any longer perceive itself as being definitively (and quasi-ontologically) right at all points, whether of doctrine, practice or ethics. This kind of absolute rightness, the Seeking Church knows, is simply not available to the church. All that is available on any given issue is a range of choices to be decided upon with much prayer, and whichever one is chosen is always thereafter subject to – or at least open to – revision.

Thus no denomination would any longer feel the need to de-

fend its own position to the uttermost, or see changing its position as a price to be paid for co-operation. Rather, all of the
churches would be pooling their very different insights on matters of doctrine and ethics and admitting the validity of all of
them. Minds may change or they may not, but in the end this is
not especially important, for the goal of this new ecumenism is
not a monolithic church where all think exactly alike, but a
church which acknowledges and rejoices in the range of possibilities of faithful belief and practice which are available, and
whilst each denomination may wish to retain its own particular
perspective, this is recognised as being a choice which might
have been different and which in no way invalidates or implies
any lack of respect for the choices of others.

Two examples might help to illustrate the kind of process
which is envisaged. First, then, the Roman Catholic Church – or
at least its hierarchy – has certain tenaciously held opinions
about the ordination of women and the celibacy of the clergy,
and it is certain that it is in some almost metaphysical and ontological sense 'right' in these opinions. This is an archetypically
Dispensing Church outlook. In the mind of a Seeking Church
these would be seen as choices – and perfectly valid ones – and
they would therefore be open to revision. The Roman Catholic
Church would listen to the rationale of other churches for ordaining women and allowing their clergy to marry, and would
come over time to a fresh estimate of its own position. In debate
it would articulate its own rationale for acting as it does and
would therefore be able to discern whether the reasons on which
these choices are based are still appropriate today or whether
they have outlived their usefulness. What it would cease doing
is simply proclaiming the rightness of its viewpoint and the consequent wrongness of the views of other churches. The Roman
Catholic Church may or may not change its corporate mind on
one or both of these issues – and indeed from the point of view
of ecumenism it does not matter very much one way or the
other, although it might matter greatly to a substantial percentage of the Roman Catholic faithful. What is important is that the

mind-set has changed regardless of the decision, and other churches' orders and practices are seen as valid although different rather than deviant.

A second pertinent example is the question of the appropriateness or even the necessity of bishops in order for a church to have a full and true ecclesial identity and order. The Roman Catholic Church, the Anglican Church and some Lutheran churches, for example, are episcopally ordered, while churches such as the Presbyterian Church and the Baptist Church are not. In discussion of the matter it can all too easily be made to seem, from the one side, that churches without bishops are not 'proper' churches, and from the other side that if, in particular, the Roman Catholic Church has bishops, then we certainly do not want them! To a Seeking Church, though, the discussion becomes much more open because again there is no sense of innate rightness involved and there is no need to defend aggressively one's chosen position. Each party is able to listen courteously to the others, respecting their stance; and just as with the Roman Catholic Church on celibacy and the ordination of women, the viewpoint of a church may or may not change. Again what is essential is that the matter is seen to lie in the realm of *adiaphora* – that is, matters on which latitude of opinion is permissible. This same principle would then also come to apply to the church's entire discussion of the different denominations' perspectives on a wide variety of issues, both ethical and doctrinal.

The second change in perspective which would ensue from the birth of a Seeking Church would concern a greatly enhanced sharing in sacraments and perhaps even of ministry. At the present time it is the openly stated position of the Roman Catholic Church at least, that there must be complete agreement over Eucharistic doctrine (by which is meant complete agreement with Roman Catholic Eucharistic doctrine) before there can be any regular Eucharistic sharing. Likewise there is no overall mutual recognition of ministries between the various denominations, with rare exceptions such as that between the signatories of the Porvoo Agreement. Both of these things would be set to change by the dawning of a Seeking Church, and again the reason lies in its openness, *agnosis* and provisionality.

Thus a Seeking Church will know its own doctrinal markers – on the eucharist as on anything else – to be partial and to be but hints and glimmers of a reality which transcends all doctrinal formulation. And again each part of the church will be open to listen to, and respect the validity of the perceptions of others, even if it does not necessarily share them. Furthermore, because all of these things are recognised as being of the second order of importance, the Seeking Church will readily acknowledge the common shared story transcending all differences of doctrinal interpretation, and will see this as the primary ground of sacramental fellowship. It will not matter unduly that there will be a variety of interpretations: what will matter is the recognition of, and rejoicing in the fact that, with Jesus and his story at the centre of things, 'all are one in Christ Jesus' (Galatians 3:28).

If each other's eucharists are recognised as valid and may therefore be shared in, then similarly, by implication the various denominations will recognise the validity of each other's ministries, acknowledging that another denomination's ordination procedure may be different, but that it is not thereby null and void. This in turn might open up the way to an interchange of ministries on occasions at least. One can readily imagine a number of situations where this might bring a very real benefit, quite apart from the joy of being able to offer to share pulpit and table on special occasions. Thus a vacancy in a parish, or clerical holidays or illness might all profitably be resourced if it were only permissible for a clergyperson of another denomination to extend the hand of friendship and offer to assist, even if only in the short term. Such a sharing would also provide a huge learning opportunity for both congregations and clergy, and new ties of respect and affection would almost certainly be forged through such practical co-operation at the local level.

A Seeking Church, if actively nurtured into life, has the potential to do for ecumenism what Aslan did for Narnia, that is, to free it from the grip of a seemingly eternal winter. And

many of the above remarks hold true for the church's 'foreign policy' also, that is, its corporate approach to the other world faiths.
Inter-faith studies, talks and praxis on the ground might all be
given a fresh impetus, direction and life if the input of Christianity
came from a Seeking rather than from a Dispensing Church.

Before going any further, one disclaimer must be issued. A
Seeking Church will not be a church which will 'sell out' its faith
or play false to it in the presence of other faiths: it is simply a
church which knows the partial and provisional nature of its
faith and believes that there is more to the 'things of God' than
we can fully know or understand; and it will therefore be open
to the spirituality, insights and wisdom of other faiths which
may have revealed glimpses of God which our own Christian
tradition has not clearly seen. Maurice Wiles expresses this acknowledgement of provisionality particularly eloquently:

> ... there are many who see themselves as orthodox Christian
> believers, but who yet conscientiously affirm the presence of
> truth in other religions. In view of the enormous differences
> of conceptuality and of beliefs between the major religions,
> there is, it seems to me, only one way in which such a posi-
> tion can be consistently maintained. If it is not to involve
> abandoning any form of realistic truth claim for religious be-
> liefs altogether, we have to acknowledge that the truth of
> those affirmations which constitute the body of Christian be-
> liefs must be of a highly partial and provisional nature. Any
> claim to certainty about the truth of one's own religious be-
> liefs is flatly incompatible with the acceptance of more than
> one religion as in any serious sense a vehicle of truth.[1]

So, then, what might a Seeking Church bring to inter-faith
dialogue and praxis which a Dispensing Church finds it hard –
or even impossible – to offer? In essence it is precisely this provisionality and openness, for these are the factors which will allow
it to listen to the voice of others, and not merely to listen, but actively to acknowledge the validity and richness of their spiritual
experience.

The effects of this for Christianity would be two-fold. First, our own faith might expect to be enriched by the experience of coming into contact with the wisdom and holiness of other faiths, whether in the structured context of inter-faith talks or in the more informal meetings, and hopefully even times of shared prayer, at a more local level. Secondly, Christianity might even be willing to revise a view or views in the light of this experience. Clearly the process would be even more fruitful if other religions also came to encounter in 'seeking' mode, but even if this is not the case, then still Christianity has much to gain from entering into the thought and prayer worlds of other faiths without bringing with it any prejudice as to the outcome, and being itself willing, if appropriate, to be shaped by the encounter. All of this was expressed with tremendous cogency some years ago by Keith Ward when he outlined his vision of an 'open theology':

> One might perhaps speak of an 'open theology', which can be characterised by six main features. It will seek a convergence of common core beliefs, clarifying the deep arguments which underlie diverse cultural traditions. It will seek to learn from contemporary beliefs in other traditions, expecting that there are forms of revelation one's own tradition does not express. It will be prepared to reinterpret its beliefs in the light of new, well-established factual and moral beliefs. It will accept the full right of diverse belief-systems to exist, as long as they do not cause avoidable injury or harm to innocent sentient beings. It will encourage a dialogue with conflicting and dissenting views, being prepared to confront its own tradition with critical questions arising out of such views. And it will try to develop a sensitivity to the historical and cultural contexts of the formulation of its own beliefs, with a preparedness to continue developing new insights in new cultural situations.[2]

All of Ward's requirements would be met by a Seeking Church.

Thus far in this chapter we have considered the ways in

which a Seeking Church might transform both the ecumenical and the inter-faith scenes, and in the context of inter-faith dialogue in particular we have reflected on the benefits which might accrue to the church from this, but there is yet one final matter to be addressed. In all inter-faith matters, then, just as with the church's dealings with the world in general, it is important that the church – a Seeking one just as much as a Dispensing one – does not forget about or renege on its commitment to sharing what it sees and experiences of the good news of God in Jesus Christ. It is, after all, subject to the great commission and promise of Matthew 28:19-20:

> Go therefore and make disciples of all nations, baptising them in the name of the Father and of the Son and of the Holy Spirit, teaching them to observe all that I have commanded you; and lo, I am with you always, to the close of the age.

At one level the church will witness to this by what it says in dialogue with other faiths, but to those of all faiths and none the Seeking Church will, I think, witness best not in words, not in deeds, not by declaiming its doctrine but by living in Christ. In an article reflecting on Pascal and his religion of the heart and not the head, Graham Tomlin expresses it appositely:

> So the first stage in a church's approach to its non-Christian neighbours ought not to be to ask 'How can we persuade them that it's true?', but 'How can we make them want to know more?'
>
> This might involve personal questions like: 'How different are my values, my home, and my behaviour from those of my neighbours who are not Christians? Is there anything there that might make them desire what I have?
>
> It might also involve an honest look at the church's lifestyle: 'Is our church just another club for like-minded people who enjoy singing, emotional trips, and funny clothes? Is there anything in the life or worship of our church that would make an outsider long for what we have?'
>
> An evangelistic life then becomes one that simply makes

other people think; that stirs a desire to find out what it is that makes the difference.[3]

Here, perhaps, is the final strength of a Seeking Church, that it is a place open enough, provisional enough and agnostic enough not to repel the uncertain or the wavering, and yet passionately Christ-centred and looking to reach out to the world not in doctrinal formulae but in the gentle power of Christ-like love and service as the stories of its members interweave with and draw strength from the story of Christ re-presented day by day in the shared fellowship of bread and wine. To have Christ at its heart and to be the heart of Christ in the world today: that is at once the nature and vocation of a Seeking Church as it proclaims a 'space for all'.

CONCLUSION

To the Future

By way of drawing this work to a close, I want to begin by addressing two possible bones of contention. First, then, to some readers, and especially to those of a more naturally conservative ecclesiastical outlook, it might seem as if I have been overly critical of the church as it at present largely exists, or that I have been 'sniping' at it by labelling it as a Dispensing Church. Such, it must emphatically be said, has not at any stage been my intention. I grew up within a church-going family, and apart from a relatively brief period of teenage rebellion my whole life has been lived within the ambit of the church. Furthermore, the church has been good to me. It has nurtured my spiritual life, exposed me to the wisdom of several valued mentors, and provided a rich support and friendship network of colleagues and parishioners. For all of these things and many more, I am, and will continue to be, most grateful.

But this gratitude, real though it is, does not take away or invalidate the need for a radical critique of the church. The fact that the church has met so many of my needs and given me so much does not automatically mean that the church, in its present manifestation, is best equipped for ministry and mission on a wider canvas. Indeed, it will have become clear that I believe that it is not so equipped. It is, in Dispensing mode, too often patronising and off-putting, and does both itself and the ministry of Christ a disservice as a consequence. And the only reason why I have felt the need to draw attention to its shortcomings and propose an alternative model of the church has been not to snipe at it but, because I love it so much, to seek to 'correct what is amiss' and empower it more completely to be Christ's presence in the world and to provide a truly Christ-like 'space for all'.

Secondly, it may be that to many this book will not look like an ecclesiology, and certainly not one of any traditional variety. I accept the criticism. It is perhaps not an ecclesiology, but it is about ecclesiology, in that it seems to me that there is a fundamental issue at stake as to the whole underlying crux of the church's self-understanding which will then inform any more formal ecclesiology which is built upon it. And these divergent self-understandings hinge on the central question of whether the church is conceived of as being some sort of repository of unchanging truth or as a people (together with their ideas and their ethics) *in via* towards a destination yet unknown. The former will suit those who see doctrine as immutable and binding; the latter will accommodate the agnostic, provisional and relational faith which has been delineated in the previous two books in this trilogy.

What has been attempted here, then, has been to set out an approach to ecclesiology: to try to establish a new way in which the church might begin to understand itself and to think about itself, and which, if pursued, might open up creative possibilities for ministry, inclusiveness and outreach. The theory of such a change is relatively simple, but the practical outworking of it is (or would be if it came fully to pass) infinitely more difficult. For there is, potentially, a huge shift to be made, and the gulf between the present reality of a Dispensing Church and the future possibility of a Seeking Church is immense. I have no illusions about the scale of the change I have proposed, nor about its realistic chances of seeing the light of day, in the short term at least. What I would contend, however, is that in the medium to longer term some such sort of shift is essential to the well-being, if not indeed the survival, of the church. The Dispensing Church appears still to be alive and well for the present, but the reality is that numbers are declining, and almost every parish of whatever denomination is finding that survival becomes ever harder year by year. At some point in the next generation or so this shrinkage will reach crisis proportions. And it will do so precisely because of the nature of the church.

In a world of widespread education, of almost countless religions and possible lifestyle choices, the church – in its widespread manifestation as the Dispensing Church at least – is in mortal danger of total irrelevance. Its attitudes and confines are too narrow, its certainties too restrictive and exclusive, and as a result ever more people are looking outside its walls for their spiritual nourishment and well-being. Increasingly the Dispensing Church will become not a vibrant kingdom-driven church, but a backward-looking refuge for the spiritually, doctrinally or ethically frightened.

In circumstances such as these, change – and far-reaching change – is not merely desirable, but essential. To say this is one thing; to bring that change about is quite another, and it will not be either easy or comfortable – birth, for churches as for human beings, is a difficult, potentially dangerous and messy business. In the short term even the first stirrings of an emerging Seeking Church will generate enormous tension, as it poses a direct threat to the entrenched self-understanding of the dominant Dispensing Church, and the Dispensing Church will, in its turn, undoubtedly fight a determined rearguard action. Looking at the Anglican Communion in particular, I believe that this is the point we have reached at the present time. There have been signs for the last generation or two that, on the part of a sizeable minority at least, attitudes are changing doctrinally, and this has been followed more recently by a willingness – on the part of a very similar minority – to revisit certain ethical issues with a view to potential revision. This is, in essence, why the current debate on homosexuality has reached such vastly over-inflated proportions, and why the tempers of lay people, clerics and not infrequently bishops have been stretched to breaking point. For people on both sides of the debate realise – whether they have articulated it clearly to themselves or not – that this debate runs far deeper than merely the issue of whether homosexual activity should be condoned or condemned, or whether homosexuals should be ordained. Beyond this superficial presenting symptom the debate takes in matters such as the authority of scripture, the means and criteria by which ethical decisions may be made and, ultimately, the church's whole sense of its own identity, boundaries and self-understanding. Small wonder that the Dispensing Church is fighting back; for it is, in a very real sense, fighting for its life.

So the process of bringing a Seeking Church to birth will not be easy, and it may not even be successful. It may be that the sheer weight of the Dispensing Church will squeeze the life out of the new born infant and stifle it, leaving the Dispensing Church temporarily triumphant and savouring, for a brief while, what will undoubtedly turn out to be a pyrrhic victory as creeping irrelevance drains its own life blood inexorably away.

If, however, the movement for change is successful and a Seeking Church comes to reality as a live birth rather than a still one, its potential for the revitalisation of both faith and church is, I believe, enormous. It is so, I suggest, in three ways especially. First, because a Seeking Church is a people *in via*, and a church aware of the provisionality of all formulations of doctrine, its members will be encouraged to think and to question rather than to stand still and thereby risk stagnation. A Dispensing Church is, covertly if not overtly, essentially inimical to thought; by contrast a Seeking Church thrives on it, as new insights are tested out and new avenues explored.

Secondly, its potential stems from its relational understanding of faith and its sense of being centred upon and gathered around a story. Its members (and quite possibly others too who may be drawn in by that story) will be enabled to relate to that story rather than merely to a set of doctrinal propositions, and encouraged to weave their own story around that central unifying story, thereby participating in a spiritual encounter which even the time-honoured statement 'I believe' cannot convey in such a living and personal fashion.

Thirdly, and flowing from this relational and personally involving understanding of faith and story, people will be encour-

aged (and enabled) to make connections between the head and
the heart and to discover what 'makes the difference'. Faith becomes less a matter of belief and acceptance of church teaching,
and more a matter of encounter and a living relationship with
God in Christ sustained by the presence of the Holy Spirit.

Finally, as well as these three 'spiritual' avenues of potential,
there is one further purely practical and pastoral one also, although it too shades into the spiritual realm also. It is a sad fact
that there would undoubtedly be a conservative hard core
which it would prove difficult, if not impossible, to reconcile to
the idea (let alone the reality) of a Seeking Church, and it must
be regretfully admitted that at least some of these people might
well find themselves unchurched by the emergence of a Seeking
Church. At the same time, however, there is a much greater
number of people who feel themselves excluded by the
Dispensing Church, or who have had vast quantities of hurt and
pain inflicted on them by the church for their perceived failings
in lifestyle, ethics or belief. With the emergence of an open, inclusive Seeking Church many of these people would, if welcomed, willingly, I think, become its members. A Seeking
Church might sadly inflict some wounds, but it would unques-
tionably have the potential to heal far more and to draw many
who currently find themselves lost or excluded into the ambit
(which is properly universal) of Christ's love.

None of the possible ways forward represents a cosy option,
but the stark reality is that the church stands at a crossroads, and
must decide whether to follow the road of change or to eschew
it. If no change is made then the Dispensing Church will continue to dispense to the increasingly few who will remain to listen.
The alternative – uncomfortable, but ultimately, I believe, life
giving – is to embrace some such sort of change as we have outlined here: a change in the entire self-understanding and self-
image of the church: to move from a Dispensing Church to a
Seeking Church. If this change is embraced then the future will
be, if uncomfortable, nonetheless dynamic: a people *in via*, journeying with God to God, and a church *sans frontières* – truly, at
last, 'a space for all'.

Notes

INTRODUCTION

1. Timothy Kinahan, *A Deep but Dazzling Darkness: A Christian Theology in an Inter-faith Perspective*, Dublin, The Columba Press, 2005, p 13.
2. Gerhard Sauter, *Gateways to Dogmatics: Reasoning Theologically for the Life of the Church*, Grand Rapids Michigan, Wm B Eerdmans Publishing Co, 2003, p 41.
3. Stephen R. White, 'Forward to the Past – A Church for the Future?' in *Being Church in the New Millennium*, Dublin, Veritas, 2000, pp 23-9, p 24.
4. Richard Henderson, *The Jealousy of Jonah*, Dublin, The Columba Press, 2006, p 10.
5. Richard Holloway, *On Forgiveness*, Edinburgh, Canongate Books, 2002, p 2.
6. As an excellent example of people doing theology in this way, and indeed, being able to articulate precisely what it is that they are doing, see, *Why I am Still a Catholic: Essays in Faith and Perseverance*, Peter Stanford (ed), London & New York, Continuum, 2005.

CHAPTER ONE

1. Mary Midgely, *The Owl of Minerva: A Memoir*, Oxford and New York, Routledge, 2005, pp 19-20.
2. Not least such luminaries as Hans Küng and Tissa Balasuriya.
3. See Stephen R. White, *A Space for Unknowing: The Place of Agnosis in Faith*, Dublin, The Columba Press, 2006.
4. Angela Hanley, 'Women and Men Doing Theology Together, *Spirituality*, Vol 12, No 64, January-February 2006, pp 24-28, p 26.
5. 'Iris Murdoch Talks to Stephen Glover', in *From a Tiny Corner in the House of Fiction: Conversations with Iris Murdoch*, ed. Gillian Dooley, Columbia, South Carolina, University of South Carolina Press, 2003, pp 33-43, p 43.
6. Tom F. Driver, *Christ in a Changing World*, London, SCM Press, 1981, p 170.
7. Marcus Braybrooke, *Explorer's Guide to Christianity*, London, Hodder and Stoughton, 1998, pp 263-4.
8. Saguna Ramanathan, Unpublished paper.

CHAPTER TWO

1. Stanley Hauerwas, *Resident Aliens: A Provocative Christian Assessment of Culture and Ministry for People who know that Something is Wrong*, Nashville, Abingdon Press, 1989. In various places the Mennonite theologian John Howard Yoder also advances a broadly similar set of ideas.

2. Stanley J. Samartha, (ed), *Living Faiths and the Ecumenical Movement*, Geneva, World Council of Churches, 1971, p 154.

CHAPTER THREE

1. Chris McVey OP, 'Steadfastness', in *Spirituality*, Vol12, No 68, September-October 2006, Dublin, Dominican Publications, pp 309-314, p 310.
2. Gerhard Sauter, *Gateways to Dogmatics: Reasoning Theologically for the Life of the Church*, Grand Rapids Michigan, Wm B Eerdmans Publishing Co, 2003, p 274.
3. See: Stephen R. White, *The Right True End of Love*, Dublin, The Columba Press, 2005.
4. Peter J. Conradi, *The Saint and the Artist: A Study of the Fiction of Iris Murdoch*, London, HarperCollins, 2001, pp 53-4.

CHAPTER FOUR

1. Stephen Sykes, *Unashamed Anglicanism*, London, Darton, Longman and Todd, 1995, p 163.
2. Sykes, p xii.
3. Timothy Kinahan, *A Deep but Dazzling Darkness*, Dublin, The Columba Press, 2005, p 29.

CHAPTER FIVE

1. Richard Kearney, *On Stories*, London & New York, Routledge, 2002, p 79.
2. Ibid., p 80.
3. Ibid., p 81.
4. Ibid., p 81.
5. Ibid., p 83.
6. Richard Kearney, *On Paul Ricoeur: The Owl of Minerva*, Hampshire, Ashgate, 2004, p 135.
7. J. L. Houlden, *Jesus: A Question of Identity*, London & New York, Continuum, 2006, pp 125 & 127.
8. Ibid., p 127.

CHAPTER SIX

1. Katie McAteer, Course Assignment, entitled 'God in the Meeting Place', from CITC Auxiliary Ministry 'Creeds' course, 2005.
2. The full text of which reads:
    Christ has no body now on earth but yours,
    No hands but yours, no feet but yours.
    Yours are the eyes through which must look out
    Christ's compassion on the world.
    Yours are the feet with which he is to go about doing good.
    Yours are the hands with which he is to bless people now.

CHAPTER SEVEN

1. I am indebted to Douglas Adams for this delightful concept as expressed in the title of one of his Dirk Gently novels, *The Long Grey Teatime of the Soul*.
2. *The Myth of God Incarnate*, ed. John Hick, London, SCM Press, 1977. This book, as might be expected from its title, contained a number of radical re-interpretations of the Incarnation, and caused something of a furore among the more conservative elements of the church in the years following its publication.
3. Albert Nolan, in *Building Bridges: Dominicans Doing Theology Together*, Dublin, Dominican Publications, 2005, p 129.
4. Mrs Bradley, retired, in 'Do people in Godley believe in the Virgin Birth?', *Guardian on Saturday*, 19 December, 1992, p 59. Quoted in, Ian Parker, *Psychoanalytic Culture: Psychoanalytic Discourse in Western Society*, London, SAGE Publications, 1997, p 68. To Mrs Bradley's words, Ian Parker adds perceptively: 'Here, religion is used as an injunction not to know. Religious ideas are the unthought which define and limit what questions might be asked, and they prevent reflection.'
5. Douglas Adams, 'Interview, American Atheists', in *The Salmon of Doubt*, London, Pan Books 2003, p 96.
6. Chapter 7 of *A Space for Unknowing*, Dublin, Columba Press, 2007.

CHAPTER NINE

1. Rachel Feldhay Brenner, 'Writing as Resistance', in *Four Women Confronting the Holocaust*, Pennsylvania, The Pennsylvania University Press, 1997, p 93.
2. Martin Lloyd Williams, *Beauty and Brokenness: Compassion and the Kingdom of God*, London, SPCK, 2007, p 31.

CHAPTER TEN

1. Victor G. Griffin, *Anglican and Irish Today: Holding the Centre*, Belfast, Catalyst, 2006, p 42.
2. Stephen R. White, *The Right True End of Love*, Dublin, The Columba Press, 2005, p 73.
3. Ibid., p 75.
4. David L. Norgard, 'Lesbian and Gay Christians and the Gay-Friendly Church', in *Our Selves, Our Souls and Bodies: Sexuality and the Household of God*, ed Charles Hefling, Boston, Massachusetts, Cowley Publications, 1996, pp 192-200, p 197.

CHAPTER ELEVEN

1. Christopher Moody, *Eccentric Ministry*, London, Darton, Longman and Todd Ltd, 1992, p 23.
2. Ibid., pp 23-4.

CHAPTER TWELVE

1. Maurice Wiles, 'Belief, Openness and Religious Commitment', in *Theology*, Vol CI, No 801, May/June 1998, pp 163-171, pp 168-9.

2. Keith Ward, *Religion and Revelation*, Oxford, Oxford University Press, 1994, p 339-40. Quoted in, Ian Markhan, 'Looking Back on the 20th Century: 3. Theological Reflections', *The Expository Times*, September 1999, pp 384-389, p 389.

3. Graham Tomlin, 'Manna to the Hungry Soul', *Church Times*, 12 September, 1997, p 15.

Index of Names

Adams, Douglas, 97.
Andersen, Hans Christian, 66.
Apollinarius, 15.
Arius, 15.
Augustine of Hippo, St, 17, 18, 146-7.

Bemanos, Georges, 148.
Bonhoeffer, Dietrich, 38.
Bradley, Mrs, 97.
Braybrooke, Marcus, 26.
Brendan the Navigator, 60.
Brenner, Rachel Feldhay, 119.

Calvin, John, 19.
Carter, Sydney, 71.
Columba, St, 60.
Conradi, Peter J., 48.
Constantine, Emperor, 14, 18.
Copernicus, Nicholas, 13.
Cyprian of Carthage, 17, 27.
Darwin, Charles, 13.

Derrida, Jacques, 39.
Diocletian, Emperor, 18.
Driver, Tom F., 25.
Dulles, Avery, 27-8, 31.

Eckhardt, Meister, 93.

Galileo, 13.
Gregory the Great, Pope, 16.
Griffin, Victor, 122-3.
Grimm, The Brothers, 66.

Hanley, Angela, 21.
Harper, Alan, 56.

Hauerwas, Stamley, 28-31, 63.
Henderson, Richard, 8.
Holloway, Richard, 9.
Houlden, J.L., 68.

Ignatius of Antioch, St, 14, 36.

Jenkins, David, 94.
John, St, 15, 59, 82-3.
John ofthe Cross, St, 93.
Jonah, 29.
Jones, Richard G., 53-4.
Justin Martyr, 15.
Kearney, Richard, 64-5.

Kinahan, Timothy, 7, 59.
Koyama, Kosuke, 63.

Lawrence, Brother, 103, 133.
Levi, 87.
Luke, St, 39, 64, 85-6, 87-8, 93.

McAteer, Katie, 80-81.
McLeod, George, 61.
McVey, Chris, 39.
Mark, St, 39, 40, 88, 89.
Matthew, St, 39, 40, 84-5, 93.
Midgeley, Mary, 13-14.
Moody, Christopher, 137, 145.
Murdoch, Iris, 25, 48.

Nero, Emperor, 18.
Nolan, Albert, 96-7.
Norgard, David L., 126-7, 131.

Okri, Ben, 64.

Paul, St, 14, 27, 33, 34, 36, 90, 91, 116.

Pelagius, 15.
Peter, St, 40, 84-5.

Ramanathan, Saguna, 26.
Ricoeur, Paul, 64-5.

Samartha, Stanley J., 34.
Sartre, Jean Paul, 48.
Sauter, Gerhard, 8, 42.
Sykes, Stephen, 52-3, 54.

Teresa of Avila, St, 83.

Tertullian, 33.
Tomlin, Graham, 158-9.

Vanier, Jean, 133.
Vincentius, 17.

Ward, Keith, 157.
Wiles, Maurice, 156.
Williams, Martin Lloyd, 119.

Zacchaeus, 87-8.